101
MOUNTAIN-BIKE ROUTES IN SCOTLAND

Other titles by the same author:

101 Bike Routes in Scotland

101

Mountain-Bike Routes in Scotland

HARRY HENNIKER

MAINSTREAM
PUBLISHING

EDINBURGH AND LONDON

Photographs © Harry Henniker and Dave McArthur
Drawings © Sally Harrower

First published in Great Britain in 1998 by
MAINSTREAM PUBLISHING COMPANY (EDINBURGH) LTD
7 Albany Street
Edinburgh EH1 3UG

ISBN 1 85158 936 8

A catalogue record for this book is available from the British Library

Maps drawn by the author using a vector graphics drawing package. Maps
manually redrawn from out-of-copyright editions of the Ordnance Survey
One Inch Map supplied in photocopied form by the National Library of
Scotland and updated by direct observation and with Garmin GPS software.
Heights on maps taken with a Thommen Altimeter.

Typeset in New Caledonia and Copperplate by Brinnoven, Livingston
Printed and bound in Great Britain by Butler & Tanner Ltd, Frome

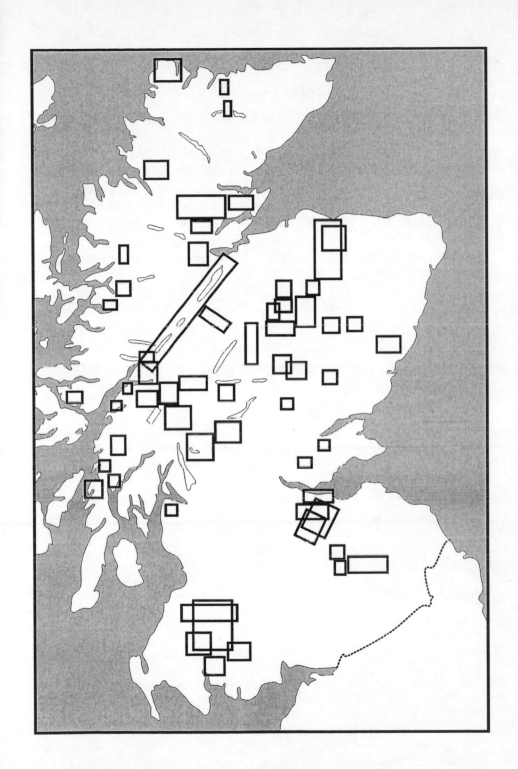

SPECIAL NOTE

Because this book covers the whole of mainland Scotland it has been necessary to include some routes that have already been described in my (mainly road-cycling) book *101 Bike Routes in Scotland*. At the next revision, the mountain-bike routes will be taken out of the earlier book and the space used instead to cover the Sustrans millennium cycle-route network in Scotland, which will be nearly complete by that date. This book (*101 Mountain-Bike Routes in Scotland*) is all mountain-biking. *101 Bike Routes in Scotland* will be about quiet roads and cycle paths. You might like to know that the bike routes in both books are also available individually as laminated cards.

CONTENTS

Acknowledgements

I'm grateful to a lot of people who've contributed in one way or another to this book, but there are three people in particular without whom it could never have happened.

The first is Sally Harrower; her brilliant cartoons appear on nearly every page. Her ability to create little pictures of mountain-bikers in response to my sometimes vague ideas about what I want is just amazing. A cycling magazine described them as inspired in a review of the last book, and she's done even better this time.

The second person I'm indebted to is Dave McArthur. His wide knowledge of the Scottish hills has introduced a lot of new bike routes, and his practical support, both on and off a bike, has been invaluable. I'm particularly grateful for his help with taking photos as we checked out many of the bike routes.

Finally I should thank my brother Dave Henniker. Without his help in setting up my computer, and coming along to solve problems which were beyond my ability to sort out, the project would hardly have got started.

INTRODUCTION

I spend a lot of time looking at bike routes. I run a bus service (the BikeBus) which takes people mountain-biking all over Scotland. I've been doing this for eight years; naturally by now I've a pretty good idea of where the best bike routes are.

Why a book covering the whole of Scotland costing £15, instead of a series of little local guides costing £6 each? Well, the idea is that if you're anywhere in mainland Scotland you can look inside and there will be several bike routes near you. All you have to do then is decide which one. The routes are graded to assist with this, and if you read the description you get more details: scenery, distance, height of climb and descent, a proper map, and what most maps and books don't tell you – a description of the surfaces you ride on.

Another advantage of a larger book is that I can tell you about long mountain-bike routes. I know that a lot of mountain-biking is done as short, circular trips with the bike hung from the back of a car, and there are plenty of routes for this in the book. I'd like to encourage you to go further. Did you know that you can bike from Fort Augustus virtually to Oban, hardly going on a public road?

This is a book for mountain-bikers, not walkers. Some guide books are described as being for walkers and mountain-bikers, but are rather vague about which routes are appropriate for mountain-biking and which are not. This neatly shifts the blame for cycling in the wrong place from the author to the mountain-biker. At the time we went to print you could ride a bike over all the routes. I know this because I've actually done it for the vast majority; a few routes have been checked out for me by friends.

A few years ago I was biking in the USA and was passing through Marin County on my way to San Francisco (having started at Seattle). I was obviously a foreigner and a mountain-biker pedalled up to me and said, hey, did I know that I was passing through the best mountain-biking territory in the whole world? I hung around the area for a few days and had to admit he had a point. All the same, he was wrong – it's Scotland.

ROUTE-GRADING SYMBOLS

Yes, the cartoons actually mean something. Of course, to get the full picture you need to read the text. For instance, the cartoon for a river crossing doesn't actually mean it's going to be exactly as depicted; all it means is that there's a river crossing which will involve at least getting your feet wet. Cartoons are sometimes used in combination to 'fine tune' the description.

All of the routes in this book are bikeable by an average rider. What does this mean exactly? It means that I'm about average, and when I went over the route I found that I could bike at least 80 per cent. If I couldn't bike 80 per cent, as far as I'm concerned it's a walking route, so it isn't in this book. Most of the routes are in fact 100 per cent bikeable, but if you're an expert or a beginner, make appropriate adjustments.

Personally, I'm far from being the most expert mountain-biker in the world. I often find that when I take competition-standard riders over routes where I walk some sections, they just bike the whole thing. Likewise, little girls who are borrowing their brother's mountain-bike for the first time tend to walk a bit more than me. I generally find that when I have school parties (12–14-year-old males, usually) they bike everywhere that I do.

EASY

Easy forest road or canal towpath; a bit bumpy only; could be ridden on any bike.

MODERATE

Good Land Rover track, average forest road or trail; not particularly hilly or technically difficult.

MORE DIFFICULT

Contains steep sections that are hard work to get up, and fast or difficult to descend.

DIFFICULT

Some hilly parts (up to 20 per cent of route) may have to be walked.

Very Difficult

Some parts (up to 20 per cent of route) will have to be walked. You will need to carry your bike for some of this.

Rocks on Route

Some flatter sections (up to 20 per cent of route) where rocks, boulders, etc. make walking necessary.

Bumpy Sections

Some parts are bumpy, but they can still be cycled over.

River Crossing

Contains a river crossing which is rocky or deep and cannot be biked over (*do not attempt to cross burns and rivers in spate*).

Might Be Muddy

Can be very muddy in wet conditions. This means you may get dirty, but you can still do it!

Road Sections

Contains some sections on public roads.

Deer-Stalking

Stalking is possible around mid-August to late September; check locally during this period.

Narrow Twisting Path

Path is narrow and twisting in places.

MAP SYMBOLS

PLANTATION FOREST

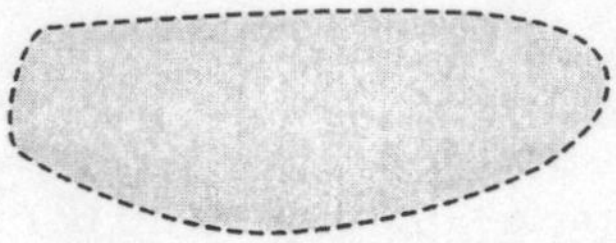

WOODLAND

FRESHWATER LOCH

SEA OR SEA-LOCH

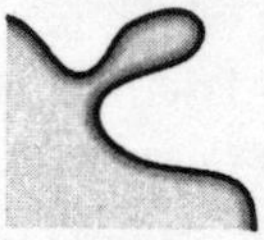

CLASS A ROAD

CLASS B ROAD

MINOR ROAD

DIRT ROAD OR TRACK

purple

blue

red

green

other track

**COLOURS OF SIGNS
ON SIGNPOSTED ROUTES
(GENERALLY DIRT TRACKS)**

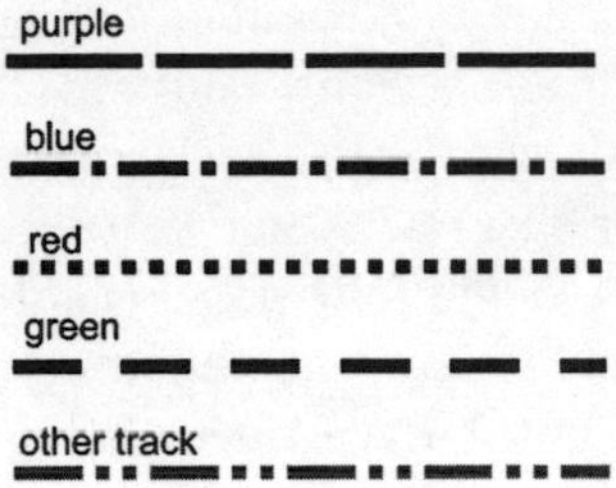

RIVER OR BURN

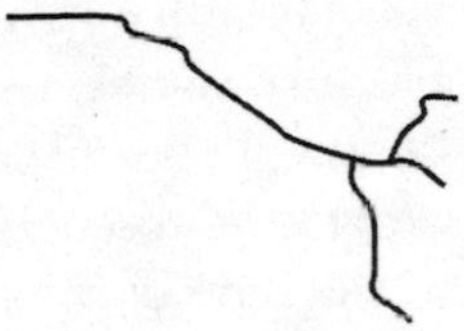

SPOT HEIGHT ON ROUTE +123M

A Ghlas
bheinn
920m

MOUNTAIN RIDGE

CLIFFS AND SCREE

CRAGS

13

How the Book Is Organised

In my opinion the mountain-biking areas in Scotland divide naturally into four different regions: Southern Scotland, Eastern Highlands, Western Highlands and Northern Highlands. Within these areas there's a wide variety of bike routes, and very often shorter day routes can be combined to make a longer tour, possibly lasting a week or more.

Mountain-biking possibilities near to the big cities are, of course, more limited, but I have nevertheless included chapters on routes near Edinburgh and Glasgow. These contain what I think are the best routes near to these cities.

Each chapter begins with a short overview. This contains a map giving the location of the bike routes, and a graphical illustration showing the routes and how they might be linked together to make longer trips. There's a brief discussion of the advantages and disadvantages of each area so that you can compare the type of mountain-biking you want to do to what's available.

The three highland areas are, of course, next to each other, so I've put in a number of off-road linking routes which might be useful if you want to do a very long off-road tour. This isn't a guide to pubs and tea rooms, but if there is a pub, tea room or youth hostel near the route, I've generally mentioned it if I think it might be useful.

Finally, the mountain-biking areas don't correspond to the Regional Areas of Scotland; the logic that connects them is biking, not government. And just in case you ask, yes, it is possible to mountain-bike on some of the Scottish Islands, but routes are fairly limited.

MOUNTAIN-BIKING IN SCOTLAND

NOTES ON LAND ACCESS

In some countries, Norway for example, you have the legal right to go anywhere in the mountains, regardless of who owns them. This is not the legal situation in Scotland.

The practical situation in Scotland is that you can wander about most places in the hills and no one will worry very much providing you don't inconvenience the landowner or cause any damage. The landowner has the right to ask you to leave (or to ask you not to enter), but in practice the vast majority of landowners have better things to do than spend a lot of time chasing away people who aren't doing any harm.

As far as land access is concerned, mountain-biking exists in a kind of limbo*; even the official mountain-bike routes weren't purpose-built. Scotland is crossed by a huge number of tracks and trails of all kinds: old military roads; forest roads; bulldozed dirt roads for shooting parties; farm tracks – the list is endless. How do you know if you're allowed to bike along them or not?

The short answer is that if there isn't a sign saying 'no bikes' (and there rarely is) and you aren't doing any harm, there isn't any reason why you shouldn't. The trouble is you might be doing damage you aren't aware of, for example frightening sheep during lambing time, or disturbing the deer-stalking. These two examples mean it's necessary to be careful at certain times of year for some routes, but it's a good idea to be well informed generally, so here are the answers to all the questions I can think of.

Scottish Rights of Way Society
Public Footpath to Glen Gordon

GLEN GORDON
ESTATES PLC
NO VEHICLES

---

* Limbo: region on the border of hell where just, pre-Christian men and unbaptised infants are confined (Concise Oxford Dictionary). Not unlike biking on a bad day!

FOREST ROADS

You can generally go anywhere you like on forest roads, providing, that is, there isn't any timber extraction or other work going on. If there is, there will be warning signs. The Forestry Commission specifically say you can use their forest roads. This applies even if they aren't signposted mountain-bike routes. You're often best to stick to signposted routes, though; otherwise you're likely to get lost.

HIGH-PLATEAU AND MOUNTAIN SUMMITS

You shouldn't be mountain-biking here at all because the damage a bike does in these areas is severe and long-lasting. Comparative repeated tests have shown that the damage a mountain-bike does in a fragile peatland area is nine times greater than a walker. The damage takes many years to repair itself in this sub-arctic environment. Needless to say, the routes in this book don't take you biking on these areas.

PUBLIC RIGHTS OF WAY

These are most commonly signposted by the Scottish Rights of Way Society, usually signposted as Public Footpath to Somewhere or Other. The signs usually say 'footpath', but the Scottish Rights of Way Society advise that there is no legal basis for discrimination between walkers and cyclists. It's in the nature of a right of way that it has to be exercised regardless of the opinion of the landowner. If you ask permission first you are not asserting your right. Of course, landowners are entitled to expect that you don't cause any damage.

UNLOCKED GATES

Gates on tracks and roads are usually to prevent animals from straying; leave them as you find them.

LOCKED GATES

You may meet these on the more difficult routes. In hill areas there's usually a side gate for walkers which is not locked; wheel your bike through this. Sometimes the pedestrian's gate is a wee bit tight for a bike, and you might need to manoeuvre it through. It's not unknown for some estates to build gates with an extremely narrow walker's gate which is nearly impossible to get a bike through.

This wasn't a problem with any of the routes here at the time of writing, but if you should encounter such a thing at the end of your ride and have to pass through, bear in mind that it's preferable to dismantle your bike rather than the gate. Most mountain-bikes have quick-release wheels and saddles; add pedals that come off easily and it should solve the problem.

PRIVATE ROAD: NO VEHICLES

A sign like this can generally be taken to mean no motor vehicles. If the landowner wanted to prohibit pedestrians and cyclists, you could expect the sign to say so.

DEER-STALKING

Because deer in Scotland have no natural predators it's necessary to reduce their numbers each year. This is done in late summer and autumn using high-powered rifles. The main problem with this is not that you are likely to be shot, but that you will disturb the deer, wasting the day of the shooting party.

Mountain-bikers who are restricted to tracks are less likely to be a problem than hill walkers who go on to the mountain ridges. The routes where this could be a problem are indicated. Ask the local tourist office if stalking is going on, or solve the problem by using another route during mid August to late September.

GROUSE-SHOOTING

The glorious 12th (of August) can sometimes be a problem for the rest of us as well as for the grouse. You can tell if you are in a grouse-shooting area by the burning of the heather. The hillside will be covered in burnt and green patches where the heather has been selectively set on fire to encourage new shoots to feed young chicks. There should be warning notices, but this shouldn't be a problem for routes in this book. A grouse shoot is a short-lived event which happens on a very limited number of days in any one area.

LAMBING SEASON

Again, most of the routes in this book are chosen to avoid this problem. If you encounter sheep during the period March to May, it's likely they will either be pregnant or with lambs. A bit of common sense is all that's needed: go round if you can; if you can't, go quietly and slowly. If you see what appears to be an abandoned lamb, leave it alone; if you touch it the mother will refuse to feed it because it will have the wrong smell.

EROSION

Mountain-bikes do cause erosion, but then so do walkers and Land Rovers. Most of the time the damage a bike does is similar to that done by a walker – virtually none when you keep to hard tracks and paths. Soft, peaty soil is where bikes do the most damage; if you have to cross an area like that, it's best to walk. The damage is, of course, greatly magnified in wet conditions; avoid fierce braking on soft, wet surfaces. The worst damage I've ever seen was caused by a group of horse-riders galloping over wet, peaty soil in the Pentland Hills – it looked like several tanks had been on manoeuvres!

FOREST OPERATIONS

If you're biking through a forest area where tree-cutting or other work is going on, there should be warning signs telling you to go somewhere else, so that's what you have to do. Occasionally, however, you might be coming off the hill, and going down the forest road is the only way out. In this situation make sure the forest workers see you and don't proceed until they wave you on. Keep well clear of stacks of logs which could roll over you if they are disturbed.

Deer Fences

These are high fences to keep deer out of certain areas, most commonly plantation forests, or where the land is being allowed to regenerate naturally for conservation reasons. The most likely situation is that you'll meet a locked gate in a deer fence, with a high stile over the fence for walkers to climb over – this is what you have to do too.

It may be easier if there are two of you and you can pass bikes over. Failing this, grasp the bike firmly in your right hand by the down tube (just above the pedals) so that the chain ring is on the outside, and use your other hand to steady yourself as you go over. Take luggage over separately; don't damage the deer fence.

Nature Trails etc.

Quite often bike routes start near nature trails or other footpaths used by families with young children. A bit of common sense is required here. Don't come up silently from behind and surprise people. Remember, *you* may know that you're not going to run into the toddler wobbling about on the path, but the anxious parents don't know you can stop in an instant. Don't give them a heart attack by pressing on regardless; they'll turn into lifelong enemies of mountain-bikers. Say something, make a joke, make it obvious you're taking care.

Mountain-Biking Code of Conduct

(Scottish Sports Council)

Think about Others

Ride with consideration for others, and give way to walkers, horse-riders and farm and forestry workers. Give friendly greetings to people you approach and thank those who give way to you. Watch your speed when close to others. Try to avoid places that are used heavily by pedestrians, especially families. Walk through congested areas; don't come up silently behind people. Respect the work of the land, avoid forestry operations, and don't disturb sheep-gathering or game-shooting.

CARE FOR THE ENVIRONMENT

Keep to hard tracks and paths; don't cut corners. Walk over soft ground. Avoid fierce braking and skidding. Don't take bikes on to fragile mountaintops and plateaux. Take litter home.

LOOK AFTER YOURSELF

Watch your speed on loose surfaces and when going downhill. Match your speed to the track surface and your skill. Scotland can be rough and remote; bike within your abilities, as an accident or a breakdown in a remote area could be serious. Take a companion in remote areas. Crossing burns and rivers in spate is dangerous. Take a map and compass and know how to navigate. Carry warm, waterproof clothing, emergency food and a lamp. Take tools and a repair kit. Wear a helmet.

GETTING READY

It's surprising how often even experienced riders neglect to make simple checks, like making sure their tyres are properly inflated. Here are a few simple checks that could save a long walk!

TYRES

Tyres should be inflated to at least 50psi, and more than this if you're not a light weight. Much of the time you'll get away with tyres that are slightly under-inflated, but as soon as you go fast over rocky ground, punctures are virtually guaranteed. Obviously tyres should be in good condition with a reasonable tread and good side walls. A common defect is that brake blocks get out of adjustment and start cutting into the tyre, thus instantly trashing your brand new tyre.

CHAINS

Chains don't last forever, and they last hardly any time at all if you don't lubricate them. In addition, pedalling a bike with a dry chain is much harder work. The best thing is purpose-designed chain lube, but any old oil will do if you haven't got this.

The bit you need to oil is the rollers or bushes in the chain; squirting vast amounts of oil at the chain might work, but just one drop on each bush will attract less dirt and do the job just as well. Chains are cheap and should be replaced before they get seriously worn, otherwise they wear out the entire drive chain, sprockets, chainrings, the lot – which is much more expensive to replace.

BRAKES

The most common failure is in the cable, and these most often fail near to the brake lever, where they curve most sharply. You can't see the cable inner wire at this point, but modern bikes have cable stops that allow you to detach the cable outer and slide the outer along. This lets you inspect parts of the cable that aren't normally visible; it also lets you lubricate it. Use grease, but if you haven't got grease use oil. Even one strand of wire broken on a cable means it's going to break very soon.

PEDALS

Mountain-bike pedals take a hard pounding; being near to the ground they take most of the knocks and dirt. Checking them regularly is worth while. Conventionally it's recommended to dismantle them and re-grease at regular intervals. I don't bother with this but simply take off the dust cap and give them a squirt of oil before every ride. It only takes a few seconds and they last for years.

HELMETS

I make no excuses for going into a lot of detail about helmets. Just a few months ago I had a cyclist crash head-first off a bridge into a burn, and where was his helmet? In his pannier! Result: he had to be taken to hospital and kept in for 24 hours. Fortunately he was lucky and there was no permanent damage, but it didn't help what started as a happy outing on a lovely sunny day.

A helmet needs to be the right size for you, and fitted properly on your head. It should be level on your head, not tilted right back. Adjust the straps at the round bits just under your ears so the helmet is level. The strap under your chin should be quite snug. It doesn't need to be tight, but you should only just be able to get food into your mouth. If you can take a big bite out of a Mars Bar with your helmet on, it's probably too loose.

Your helmet needs to be comfortable or you're going to be reluctant to wear it. The most common problem is that it gets too hot. Choose a good design with lots of ventilation. The price of helmets has come down a lot recently, so there's no excuse for not having one. When you buy a helmet go to a shop that has lots of different ones you can try on, and take plenty of time making sure you get the right one. If you damage it, replace it – you can't replace your head!

CLOTHING

Specialist cycling clothing is a bit of a fashion item nowadays, but that shouldn't blind you to the fact that it's also very practical. You can bike in ordinary shorts or whatever, but jeans are a bad idea. The hard seam under your bum will be uncomfortable after a while, they restrict movement and they are horrible if they get wet. Cycling shorts which have extra padding will tend to save your backside.

Whatever kind of fabric you're sitting on, if you're biking for several days it's important that it's clean. Any professional rider who's in the saddle day after day will tell you that the hygiene of his backside needs special attention. Cycling mitts are supposed to help prevent numb hands, but I've never found them effective; far more important is your riding position. They do save your hands, though, if you have a minor spill.

RIDING POSITION

Mountain-bike frames are much more 'one-size-fits-all' than other frames, so unless you have the wrong size of bike you should be able to achieve a good riding position. Assuming you've got the right size of bike the only other variables are saddle position and handlebar position. Mountain-bikes usually have quick-release seat pins so that you can quickly adjust saddle height for going uphill. When going uphill your leg should be nearly fully extended at the bottom of its stroke.

Handlebar position comes down to height and reach (distance from saddle to bars). Not everyone realises that you can vary the position of a saddle by loosening the bolt and sliding it back or forward on its rails. You can make minor adjustments to the reach by doing this. If this isn't enough the only solution is to get a longer or shorter stem (the bit that holds the handlebar). Bar ends, which give you more variety of riding position, are a good idea, but don't use them in situations where you might need to get to the brakes quickly. For a more detailed look at problems relating to riding position, see 'Be Comfortable with your Bike'.

WHAT TO TAKE WITH YOU

If you're sure you're only going a few miles, maybe it matters less. If you're doing more than that you need to take some things, and they fall into three categories: extra clothing, emergency tools and provisions.

EXTRA CLOTHING

There was a time in Scotland when, if you were going anywhere in the hills, you were expected to wear a green cagoule. The idea was that you would then be invisible and the mountains would seem empty. Fashion has put paid to that – you'd be hard put to find a green cagoule now anywhere outside an army surplus store.

You do need a jacket, though, or at least some form of waterproof clothing. The main characteristic of Scotland's weather is its changeability; it might be warm and sunny when you set out, but Atlantic depressions can sweep in very suddenly. If you are a few hundred feet higher a couple of hours later and the weather changes, things could get very nasty indeed.

Don't rely on your ability to bike out of trouble; a mechanical problem could put paid to that and turn a one-hour cycle into a four-hour walk. You don't need anything fancy in summer, just a light waterproof jacket, but it must *be* water-proof. You also need something more than just a T-shirt to put under it.

Outside June to September, or on longer trips, protective clothing needs to be more comprehensive. Again it can be reasonably lightweight, but it will need to be able to keep you warm and dry in colder, wetter situations. How fit you are has some relevance here. You can help keep warm by exercising, but if you are unfit exercising will make you tired quickly, so you will need to rest and be able to keep warm at the same time.

You lose a third of all heat from your head; a woolly hat is easy to carry. If your jacket has a hood as well you're on the way to making yourself safer. Gloves are light and add a lot to comfort on cold days. Having wet feet on a warm day is no problem; having wet feet on a cold day can be miserable. Sometimes you can't keep your feet dry; wearing shoes one size larger than normal and two pairs of wool socks can work wonders for your comfort if you have wet feet.

If you're going mountain-biking in winter, and doing it in the hills, you need to be as fully equipped as any mountaineer, with full thermal clothing, water-proof overtrousers, a bivvy bag and so on. Needless to say, if you're doing an adventurous trip at any time of year, you shouldn't do it on your own.

EMERGENCY TOOLS

Many people carry multi-tools, a sort of cyclist's Swiss army knife, instead of carrying spanners and all the rest separately. Multi-tools have improved a lot recently, but whatever tools you carry, they need to be appropriate to the bike you're riding. Bike manufacturers have done a lot to standardise on set sizes of allen keys etc., which reduces the number of tools you need to carry. All the same, you need to look at your bike closely to see how things come apart before you can decide what to take.

There are certain things you should have. I'm discussing them as individual tools, but if your multi-tool incorporates this element that's fine. Bear in mind, though, that a multi-tool is only one tool; if you need to hold both ends of a nut and bolt, you can't do it with one tool, however sophisticated it is!

BICYCLE PUMP

'Can I borrow your bicycle pump?'
'I didn't bring it – I thought you had one.'

TYRE LEVERS

Three tyre levers is best, two is enough; plastic ones are fine for mountain-bikes.

ALLEN KEYS

These are little 'L'-shaped pieces of steel with a hexagonal cross section. If you're lucky you'll be able to take apart virtually everything on your bike using just two or three sizes (4mm, 5mm and 6mm). In all probability, though, you'll have a few bolt-on goodies which spoil this nice neat system, so you'll need to carry the next items, which are . . .

SPANNERS

Many people carry a small adjustable spanner. It might be, though, that just one ordinary spanner is enough for you. Only the very cheapest bikes nowadays need a spanner to take a wheel off, but you do need the kit to tighten up a loose pedal, and this is invariably a spanner. It's a good idea to be able to tighten a loose crank; on older bikes this is a box spanner (or crank tool), on modern bikes it's an allen key.

CHAIN TOOL

You aren't pedalling anywhere if your chain breaks, but if you've got a chain tool you can fix any broken chain in a minute or two. Beginners are the people most likely to need a chain tool, as they tend to crash gear changes; they're also the people least likely to have one. If you meet a beginner with a broken chain and you fix it for him, you'll be treated with awe and gratitude.

Chains break because they are twisted excessively in crashingly brutal gear changes, or because they are so worn that they are a disaster waiting to happen. The plates twist, a rivet pops out and you find the chain lying on the ground five yards back. All a chain tool is is a rivet extractor.

You can't repair the damaged link because it's, well, damaged. What you have to do is shorten the chain by two links (links go in pairs), then rejoin it with a good rivet. This is where the extraction bit comes in.

Put the chain in the chain tool and turn the handle so that it slowly pushes the rivet sideways. Completely remove the damaged links by pushing the rivet through completely. Having done that, you've got a broken chain with a good link at each end.

Now what you have to do is partly remove a good rivet so you can pop two good links together. Don't push the rivet out completely or you'll never get it back in again; only do it enough so that you can clip the two ends together. After this you push the good rivet back into place using the chain tool from the other side.

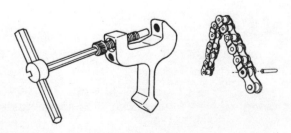

OK, the chain is shorter, but 98 per cent of the time it's too long anyway and the derailleur takes up the slack. Chains have over 100 links, so if you mess it up first time it doesn't matter. In fact, even if you take four attempts to get it right, and lose six links in the process, the chain will still be too long 94 per cent of the time – just keep off the big ring until you get home.

Puncture Repair Kit

Traditionally this is rubber solution, patches, a bit of sandpaper and some French chalk. You also get self-stick patches nowadays. The mistake beginners make is not removing the original cause of the puncture. If the thorn or whatever is still in the tyre, your repair, however beautifully done, will be very short-lived. This equally applies if you solve the problem with a new inner tube. It's a very good idea to have a spare inner tube, incidentally. You don't need a bowl of water to find the hole – just pump lots more air in, and you'll find it eventually.

Spoke Keys

Spoke keys are tiny, so carrying them is easy. Don't attempt to use them, though, unless you know exactly what you're doing. You can destroy a wheel in a minute or two by turning things the wrong way; wheel-building is beyond the scope of this book.

Bike Lock

A bike lock is an emergency tool too because it's a real emergency if someone nicks your bike! The more expensive and super-light your bike is, the more you need to carry a big, heavy bike lock. Outside the cities the problem is less acute and something lighter will do. If you're in a group, one bike lock can secure several bikes. At the end of the day in the pub or tea room, you'll enjoy your refreshment much more if you're not fretting about your bike being stolen.

Provisions

One of the great things about mountain-biking is that you can eat vast quantities of food without getting fat. In fact, you *have* to keep eating or you'll get the affliction cyclists call 'the bonk' and will collapse in a rubbery heap of jelly. One good thing about Scottish mountains is that they're not covered in cafés and après-ski establishments, but this does mean that you have to carry your own food and drink with you.

Food

When you're biking, the most important thing is to maintain a constant blood sugar level. Providing you're fit and you had a good breakfast, you'll be able to bike for several hours without running into trouble. Eventually, though, the stored glycogen in your muscles starts to run down and you feel a craving for something to eat, preferably something sweet. The answer to this problem is an early lunch.

Lunch should have a high proportion of carbohydrate (bread, cakes, fruit, honey), because that's what the body uses to replenish the energy in your muscles. In fact, the amount of energy your muscles can store is quite limited, so if you're biking very hard you need to snack constantly. If you're rolling along at an easier pace, and bike long distances regularly, you won't need to use the stored muscle energy much; you can run on fat resources instead. Eating fat won't do you any good on the day, as it takes too long to digest.

There are certain products, such as 'power bars', that are specially designed to meet the above requirements, but it's an expensive way of getting energy. A banana will do everything for you that a power bar will, and it comes in a handy package too. Chocolate is OK, but the fat in the chocolate won't do anything for you; you'll just be getting sugar. Take what you like but be sure to take enough; you need to cover your requirements, plus something for an emergency. You need more in winter.

DRINK

Scotland doesn't get the high temperatures that make this a big problem, but you still need to keep your fluid balance right. The daily demand for normal activity is between 2.5 and 3.5 litres. If you're mountain-biking hard in hot weather you could lose up to 10 litres a day, mostly as sweat. If you lose 2 per cent of your body fluid, endurance falls away; 6 per cent is serious; 12 per cent and you're dead!

Nobody need ever die from lack of water in Scotland. It's never far away and, unlike in many other countries, water from mountain streams is generally safe to drink. I carry a water bottle, of course, but often throw the contents away and replenish it from a nice cool mountain stream. Water from lochs and rivers might be OK too, but I wouldn't rely on it.

The only problem is that when you sweat you don't sweat pure water but lose minerals as well, and these need to be replaced too. Drinking pure water, tea or Coke does nothing for this. Sports drinks are specially designed to solve this problem, but fruit juice can be as good. Including some fruit (bananas again) in your lunch will solve the problem too.

Whatever type of fluid you use, it should ideally be taken in frequent small doses, and it shouldn't be chilled. Alcohol is a diuretic, i.e. it causes you to pee more fluid than you drink. Drinking lots of beer on a hot day just makes you more thirsty (and a lot more likely to crash). This is good news for the brewers but it does nothing for your fluid balance – quite the reverse.

Be Comfortable with your Bike

Doing any activity, even sitting at home, involves some risk. I'm not sure whether mountain-biking is more dangerous than sitting at home, but the health benefits balance out anyway. Increased fitness, lowered risk of heart attack, shedding excess weight, reducing stress – these are just a few of the proven benefits. Even cycling in heavy traffic is more likely to extend your life than to shorten it; statistically a cycling death only occurs every 17 million kilometres.

If you watch a group of experienced mountain-bikers it's very obvious that they're totally integrated with their machines. That's part of the seductive appeal of mountain-biking – the click-shift and the pedals almost become a part of you, and together you can just eat up terrain and fly over the ground. Being comfortable means being able to solve the problem. Regardless of whether it's an insect attack or a sore back, if you know what to do you can get back to enjoying your day.

INSECT ATTACK

Problem: Midges, small biting insects that get in your hair and eyes.
Cause: The removal of Scotland's natural tree cover over many centuries has caused the midge population to explode.
Solutions: Don't stop cycling, as you'll be going too fast for them to land on you. Wear wrap-around style sunglasses. If you stop, try to pick a breezy place. If there is no breezy place, cover up and use insect repellent.

LOWER BACK

Problems: Stiffness; soreness.
Causes: Leaning over the handlebars for extended periods. Handlebar too low in relation to saddle. Too long a stem. Leg length unequal.
Solutions: Stretch before each ride. Vary your riding position by using bar ends. Do bent-knee sit-ups to strengthen the muscles that support the spine. Raise the handlebars, making them higher or nearer as appropriate; this may mean buying a different size of stem. If you have one short leg, use a shoe insert.

HANDS

Problem: Numbness and loss of grip strength.
Cause: Excessive pressure on the handlebars.
Solutions: Wear cycling gloves with padded palms; fit bar ends to allow you to change position frequently.

EYES

Problems: Watering; dryness; itching.
Causes: Pollen. Wind penetration. UV radiation.
Solutions: Wear wrap-around style sunglasses. Wash your face frequently. Use a non-drowsy type anti-histamine.

FEET

Problems: Numbness; cold.
Causes: Shoes too small. Socks too thick for shoes. Hard plastic soles. Tight toe straps.
Solutions: Get bigger shoes, if necessary extra big to allow thick socks. Loosen shoe laces. Use an insole. Loosen toe straps. Get a different type of pedal.

SHOULDERS

Problems: Stiffness; soreness.
Causes: Insufficient handlebar reach or height.
Solution: Fit a different stem.

NECK

Problems: Stiffness; soreness.
Causes: Stationary head position. Riding position too low.
Solutions: Get bar ends to vary your riding position. Raise the handlebars with a different stem.

BUTTOCKS

Problems: Discomfort; chafing; saddle sores.
Causes: Insufficient time in the saddle. A saddle that is too narrow or too wide. Incorrect saddle height. Incorrect clothing. Didn't change your underwear.
Solutions: Ride your bike a bit more to get acclimatised or give up mountain-biking. Get a different saddle (women may need a wider saddle). Set the height correctly. Buy cycling shorts. Wear clean underpants and wash more frequently.

KNEES

Problems: Stiffness; aches; pain.
Causes: Pedalling in too high a gear. Doing too much too suddenly. Wearing cycling shorts in cold weather. Saddle too low.
Solutions: Pedal more quickly in a lower gear. Increase your daily distances slowly at the start of the season. Wear woolly tights in cold weather. Raise your saddle.

HIPS

Problem: Chronic soreness.
Causes: Incorrect saddle height. Unequal leg length.
Solutions: Adjust saddle height. Wear a shoe insert.

SKIN

Problems: Sunburn; insect bites.
Causes: Overexposure to UV radiation. Midges.
Solutions: Use a sun cream with a high protection factor. Cover burned areas with clothing. See under 'Insect Attack'.

Serious Injury

Problems: Broken limbs; head injury.

Causes: Lack of attention. Investigating odd noises in your bike while riding. Not noticing loose surfaces. Going fast at bends and blind corners. Brakes not working properly.

Solutions: Take a first-aid course. Be more careful. Fix your bike. Wear a helmet.

ROUTES IN SOUTHERN SCOTLAND

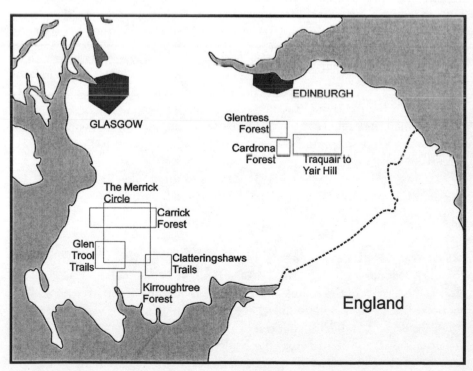

OVERVIEW

The routes in Southern Scotland are mostly in forests, but they are surprisingly varied. Often there are fine open views and there are plenty of interesting more technical routes, as well as easier ones for children.

Another advantage of Southern Scotland is that it's often very quiet, Dumfries and Galloway particularly so. There are a vast number of routes in Galloway Forest Park. Many of them are signposted but it's not necessary to stick to these, and I have some suggestions for longer, more difficult routes in this area.

The best routes in the Scottish Borders are in the Valley of the River Tweed. The hills here are steep-sided, but there are some great routes along the ridges with long scenic views and fast descents. The small mill towns along the River Tweed have plenty of cosy pubs and tea rooms to finish in at the end of the day.

None of the routes in Southern Scotland have any restrictions due to deer-stalking or grouse-shooting. It will be immediately obvious, however, that there are a lot of sheep. If you should pass through a field of sheep, remember that they will be pregnant or with lambs during February to April; go slowly and carefully.

GLEN TROOL FOREST TRAILS

Four easy mountain-bike routes in scenic Glen Trool.

INTRODUCTION

The Forestry Commission has created four mountain-bike routes in Glen Trool, all starting from Glen Trool Visitor Centre. Please bear in mind that forestry operations may mean that some sections are occasionally closed.

There is a tea room in the visitor centre, and a notice board describing the trails on the other side of the road. Further up the glen there is an attractive camp site with a shop, and there is a hotel serving bar food just south of Glentrool Village.

The town of Newton Stewart is eight miles south of Glen Trool. A good way to reach this on a bike is via the quiet minor road starting from Borgan (see map).

MINNIWICK ROUTE
(5 miles, red markers)

This is the easiest of the routes; most of it is on quiet minor roads with a forest section of just over a mile to link these up. The few hills are very gentle. The route would be suitable for children provided they were supervised.

From the visitor centre cross the bridge over the Water of Minnoch, then turn left. This road runs south-west through the forest for two miles. Ignore the left turn for Borgan but look out for a red marker post indicating a right turn to a forest trail.

Follow this trail for just over a mile, then turn right again. Pass a hotel, then Glentrool Village, then turn right again to return to the visitor centre.

BORGAN ROUTE

(10 miles, purple markers)

About half of this route is on dirt roads, with the remainder on quiet minor roads. The dirt-road section has the occasional climb and fast descent; the higher sections have good views over Bog Wood and the Water of Trool.

Begin at the visitor centre and turn left, taking the minor road east up Glen Trool. After one and a half miles turn right towards the camp site, cross the Water of Trool, then look out for a purple marker post and bear right on to the forest road.

There are some ups and downs over the next two miles, but overall there is a climb of 100 metres. Following this there is an elevated section with good views, then a fast descent to the minor road at Borgan. Turn right here, then right at the next junction to return to the visitor centre.

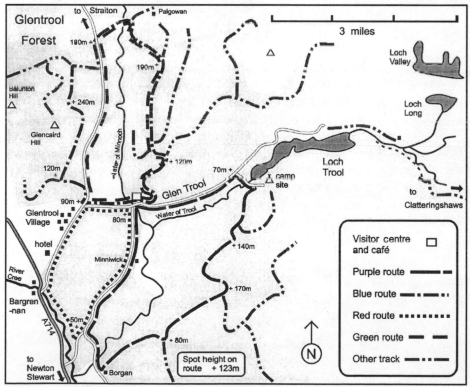

PALGOWAN ROUTE
(8 miles, green markers)

This route heads north from the visitor centre. Some climbing is involved but the gradients are fairly gentle. It's probably easiest to do the route in a clockwise direction, as this means you do the climb on a tarmac surface, with a downhill return to the visitor centre on forest roads.

Turn right from the visitor centre, crossing the Water of Minnoch, heading towards Glentrool Village. Turn right at the T-junction to the north of the village and head uphill on the minor road for about three miles.

At an open area you pass a left turn marked with a blue marker post. Ignore this but shortly after turn right towards Palgowan, following the green marker. After crossing the Water of Minnoch bear right.

Following this there is a gradual climb to a T-junction where you turn right, then a long descent over three miles all the way to the visitor centre.

Keep an eye out for the green marker posts, as there are a few more turns to make. If you find yourself going seriously uphill you have taken a wrong turning.

BALUNTON HILL ROUTE
(9 miles, blue markers)

This is the same as the Palgowan Route except that there is a further extension west towards Balunton Hill.

Why the Forestry Commission have called this the Balunton Hill Route is a bit of a mystery, for the route actually passes far closer to Glencaird Hill. Whatever the name, however, this part of the route offers good views over Glen Trool.

There's a height difference of 120 metres over a mile as you go round Glencaird Hill, which is great if you're going south, but a bit of a plod travelling north. For this reason I'd prefer to do the route in an anti-clockwise direction, as the climb on the east side is gentler.

There are other mountain-bike routes at Clatteringshaws Loch, about eight miles east of here (see following pages).

KIRROUGHTREE FOREST

A small forest near Newton Stewart; hilly, good views.

INTRODUCTION

The hills in this fairly compact forest tend to be short but steep, but once you are up there you are often rewarded with a fine view. Many of the trees here are quite large as planting began here in 1921, just two years after the Forestry

Commission was started with the aim of making Britain more self-sufficient in timber.

This forest forms a small part of the much larger Galloway Forest Park. All the local routes begin at the visitor centre; this has a tea room and a set of displays illustrating the development of forestry in the UK.

The routes are all on forest (dirt) roads with some sections on public roads. This may include the A712 (which is fairly quiet).

PALNURE BURN ROUTE
(4 miles, blue markers)

This isn't really a mountain-bike route at all as it's entirely on public roads. Still, if you're looking for an easy potter with a small child this should be suitable, as it's fairly flat.

Turn left from the visitor centre and continue following the blue markers. The route is shared with the red and purple routes for the first two miles.

DALLASH ROUTE
(10 miles, purple markers)

This route goes round the perimeter of the forest, beginning with a gradual climb up by Palnure Burn to Bargaly Glen. At the top of the Glen it turns south-west, initially on a forest road. After this it joins the A712 for two miles, then re-enters the forest to join the green route to return to the start.

Begin at the visitor centre, turning left towards the minor road to the south. Turn left again on to this road, then, after 500 metres, at the next crossroads turn left again to travel north with Palnure Burn on your right.

Continue north for four miles; the easy blue route leaves you after just over a mile, turning right to cross Palnure Burn. The purple route continues north on a forest road, following red and purple markers.

Turn left at a T-junction just after the houses at Dallash. A steep climb follows, then turn left again at the next junction (the red route continues straight on here).

Following this the climb is more gentle, eventually levelling off. Continue south-west for about a mile, then swing north to join the A712.

The two-mile section on the A712 is mostly a descent, so you will not be on it for very long. Watch out for the purple (and red) marker post showing where you re-enter the forest.

Following this there is another right turn, then you meet the green route; you turn right on to this, and then follow green, purple and red markers back to the visitor centre. The final section is a fast descent on a minor road.

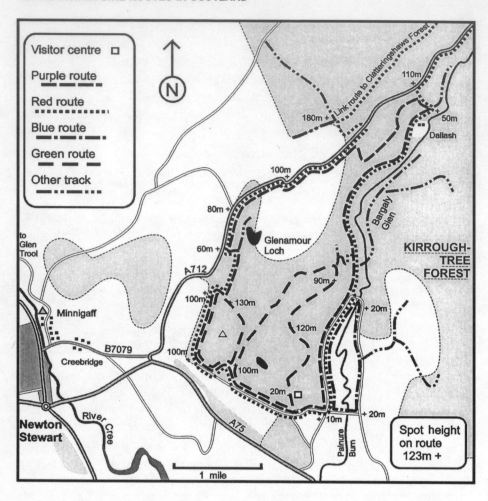

OLD EDINBURGH ROUTE

(18 miles, red markers)

This route is essentially the same as the purple route except that it includes a linking section to the north which connects to more bike routes at Clatteringshaws Forest. The linking section runs north for four miles on a forest road where it meets the Clatteringshaws purple and blue routes.

The Kirroughtree red route uses the A712 to return to Kirroughtree Forest, where it rejoins the purple route to complete its circle. The route is named after the Old Edinburgh Road (now a forest dirt road) which it follows to complete the link.

LARG HILL ROUTE

(7 miles, green markers)

This route forms a figure of eight, going round Larg Hill on the west side. Whichever way you go round there's a steady climb from the visitor centre. Once you are up there, though, you tend to stay at a high level, with good views and easier gradients.

You might prefer to begin by travelling west on the minor road from the visitor centre, as that way you get to do much of the climb on a tarmac surface.

AROUND CLATTERINGSHAWS LOCH

Good for families, with fine views – and a tea room too!

INTRODUCTION

The routes here have Clatteringshaws Loch as their focal point and offer good views of the loch and the Galloway hills. Near to the loch and the A712 is Clatteringshaws Forest Wildlife Centre. This has a tea room and a set of high-quality displays illustrating local wildlife. This area is well known for wild goats, and red deer are also common.

One of the forest routes, the Raider's Road, is promoted as a forest drive. The Forestry Commission leaflet also suggests using this as a bike route. For me, one of the main attractions of off-road biking is that there are no cars, so this would not be top of my list. However, there is a wide choice of other routes available.

The routes, if followed singly, involve some cycling on the A712. It's possible to avoid this by doing a blue/purple circuit (see map); however, the A712 is fairly quiet.

CLATTERINGSHAWS LOCH ROUTE

(14 miles, green markers)

This is one of the most scenic routes, as it goes round the loch. Turn left from the visitor centre and bike north-east on the A712 for about a mile. Turn left again on to a narrow road at the green marker post.

This road climbs gently uphill for two miles. Ignore the first left turn after a mile but take the left turn after this to enter forest on a dirt road. This descends to the loch side, then follows the River Dee.

After a further three miles turn left, cross the river and climb to a T-junction; turn left here. After a brief climb there is a fast descent over a mile to another junction, where you meet the purple route; turn left again here.

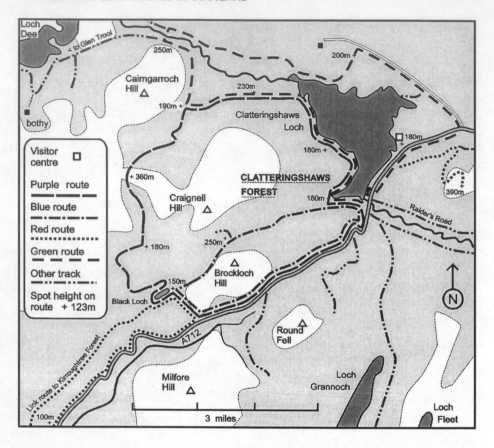

By now you will be on a surfaced road again. Follow this back to the loch, then follow the loch shore back to the public road. Turn left on to the A712 to return to the visitor centre.

CRAIGNELL HILL ROUTE
(15 miles, purple markers)

This route involves some climbing, but you are well rewarded by fast descents and good views.

Start at the access road at the south end of Clatteringshaws Loch; this is one mile south of the visitor centre. Follow the purple marker post to enter the forest. The first four miles are on a tarmac surface; this ends near where the green and purple routes diverge. Turn left at this point.

From here there is a steady climb over a mile and a half as the route travels south-west to get round Craignell Hill. You pass some open areas with the crags of Milfore Hill on your right.

There is a fast descent, then some further ups and downs. You go round Black Loch and meet the red route, where you turn left. When you meet the blue route, turn right to return to the A712.

DEER RANGE ROUTE

(9 miles, blue markers)

This is a slightly more difficult route following the Old Edinburgh Road, now a forest track. Return is on the A712. The route is best done anti-clockwise, as this ensures the steep off-road section is a descent.

Again start at the access road at the south end of Clatteringshaws Loch, but keep left this time, following blue markers. There is a gentle climb over a mile and a half to the summit at 250 metres, then a steep descent to where the routes merge near Black Loch. Turn left here to return to the A712.

BENNIGUINEA HILL ROUTE
(4 miles, red markers)

This is a 200-metre climb over two miles, followed by a return the way you came.

The view from the top is pretty good, and if you like fast descents this is a good one. Otherwise it's: 'Why do we have to climb to the top of this hill, Dad, if we're just going to come down again?'

LINK ROUTES TO OTHER AREAS

There are other marked mountain-bike routes in Glen Trool Forest and Kirroughtree Forest. These can be reached on the link routes shown on the map. The link route to Glen Trool follows part of the Southern Upland Way; follow signs with the thistle symbol. You will need to walk for about a mile.

CARRICK FOREST

A long route in Galloway Forest Park, from Barr in Ayrshire to Loch Doon; various circular options.

GENERAL NOTES

This route is at high level much of the way, so it has good views. The waymarked route is not circular, but quiet roads create circular options. It runs from the village of Barr in Ayrshire and reaches Dumfries and Galloway at Loch Doon, a total distance of 20 miles. The hills are steeper at the east (Barr) end of the route.

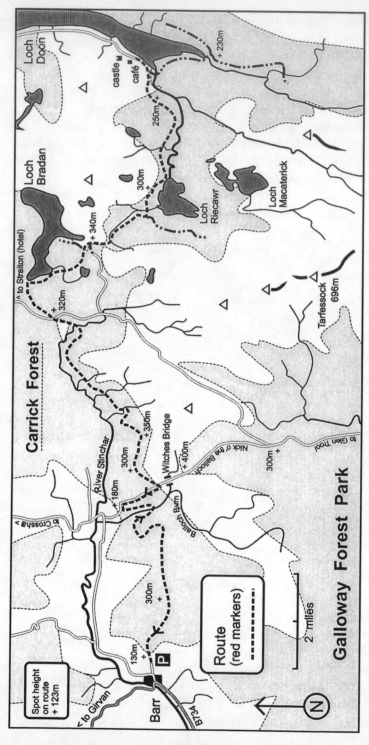

There is a good pub at Barr, and a tea room and a hotel serving excellent meals at Straiton (off map to the north).

The Banks and Braes o' Bonny Doon are still as lovely as when Robert Burns sang of them, though no doubt they are now a little changed. While the route finishes at Loch Doon, the nearest river most of the time is in fact the River Stinchar.

If you have to return to a car you may choose to bike the route in both directions. Other alternatives are to join or leave the route at the two public roads that bisect it, the Straiton to Glen Trool road or the Crosshill to Glen Trool road. You can also return from a minor road just south of Loch Bradan.

Returning to Barr using the minor road via the River Stinchar is quite easy. The other suggested circular routes use the hilly Nick o' the Balloch road.

BARR TO BALLOCH BURN

(6 miles one way)
(10 miles circular)
Start in the village of Barr, which is five miles east of Girvan. In the village, bike east away from the river; the forest entry is a left turn after half a mile. The route is marked with red marker posts.

The first two miles are a steady climb to the top of Balloch Hill, after which there is a very steep descent, crossing Balloch Burn at the bottom. After crossing the burn there is a sharp left bend to turn north.

After biking north for half a mile you have the option of returning on the minor road by the River Stinchar. To do this, turn left then left again, crossing the Balloch Burn but keeping on the south bank of the River Stinchar; the circular distance is 10 miles.

To continue on the main route, bear right to follow the route as it doubles back on itself, climbing steeply south on the Nick o' the Balloch minor road.

After a mile, as you leave the forest, turn sharp left to go round Pinbreck Hill on a forest road. If you meet a bridge over the burn (Witches Bridge), you have gone too far.

BALLOCH BURN TO LOCH BRADAN

(8 miles one way)
(25 or 28 miles circular from Barr)
The route follows the contour along the edge of the hill giving fine views, the river far below. After passing Black Hill it crosses the Straiton to Glen Trool road, two miles west of Loch Bradan.

Here you again have the option of making a 25-mile circular route using the public road. Turn south for five miles, turning north again to the Nick o' the Balloch road near a picnic site. This option involves a big climb in either direction.

To continue to Loch Bradan follow the marked route east. There is a good picnic site with a fine view at Loch Bradan. Just after this you again have the option of turning right to do a 28-mile circular route by joining a minor road just south of Loch Bradan (see map).

LOCH BRADAN TO LOCH DOON

(6 miles one way)

Continuing to Loch Doon is mostly a gentle downhill ride. On the way you pass pretty Loch Riecawr, which also has picnic tables. The route ends near Loch Doon Castle. This was re-erected on the shore when the loch was enlarged.

Just before the castle there is a bike-hire shop which doubles as a tea room and also sells craft products. The owner was able to sell me a replacement brake cable.

The route between Loch Riecawr and Loch Doon is also a forest drive, so there may be the occasional car.

THE MERRICK CIRCLE

46 miles in Galloway Forest Park.

INTRODUCTION

If you've never biked in this area before, get ready to be surprised!

Galloway Forest covers a huge area and has a big variety of scenery. OK, the mountains aren't as high as in the highlands, but you wouldn't know it by looking at them. A big plus is that Galloway is just so quiet.

This route is quite long and you might prefer to do it over two days, possibly staying at one of the two bothies (rough shelters) *en route*. You could miss out the road section if you have a non-cycling driver.

Most of the route is on Land Rover track, but there are two parts of just over a mile on footpath, which you may need to walk.

GLEN TROOL
VISITOR CENTRE
TO LOCH DEE

(8 miles)

Start at the visitor centre in Glen Trool (where there are toilets, a car park and a café). Continue up Glen Trool to the end of the road.

At the end of the public road continue along the stony track, which plunges steeply. Cross a little bridge near a waterfall. The track drops steeply again to loch level. Go over a bridge and enter oak woods.

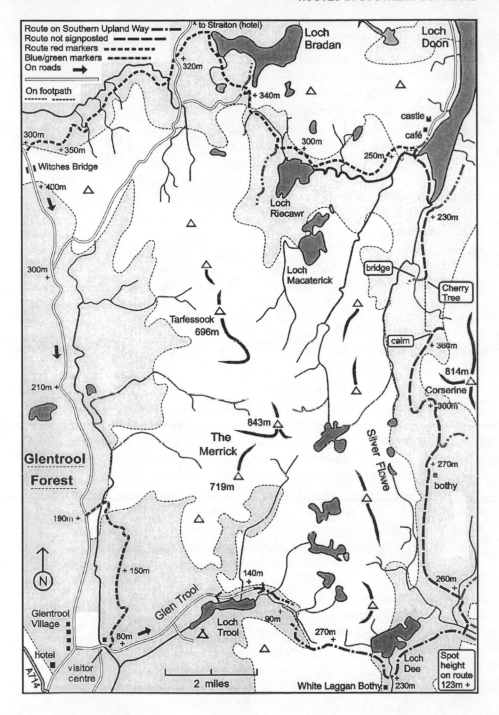

Route on Southern Upland Way
Route not signposted
Route red markers
Blue/green markers
On roads
On footpath

to Straiton (hotel)

Loch Bradan

Loch Doon

+320m

+340m

300m
+350m

300m

Witches Bridge

+400m

250m

castle
café

+230m

Loch Riecawr

300m

bridge

Cherry Tree

Loch Macaterick

300m

cairn

+360m

210m +

814m

Corserine

+300m

Tarfessock
696m

843m

270m

The Merrick

bothy

Silver Flowe

719m

Glentrool Forest

190m +

260m

150m

140m

N

Glen Trool

90m

Glentrool Village

Loch Trool

270m

hotel

80m

A714

visitor centre

2 miles

Loch Dee

White Laggan Bothy

230m

Spot height on route
123m +

Shortly after, look for a waymark sign. Leave the track and bike towards the stream on your right (Glenhead Burn). If you meet a cottage and corrugated iron outbuildings, you have gone too far.

At the burn, go upstream to a footbridge. Cross the burn and then turn left, continuing upstream on a footpath. Cross two stiles and enter plantation forest. Continue until you reach a forest road, where you turn left.

Bike uphill to emerge from the forest by a gate and continue climbing to a concrete bridge. After this there is a descent, with views over Loch Dee towards the Silver Flowe. At the end of this you enter a more open forest area, then cross White Laggan Burn. The bothy is a little way upstream on a footpath. Most bothy users will be walkers doing the Southern Upland Way.

LOCH DEE TO LOCH DOON
(14 miles)

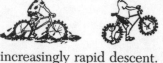

After Loch Dee there is a further climb, then an increasingly rapid descent. Look out for a circular stone sheep pen on your left; turn left here to cross the River Dee. Immediately after crossing the river, turn left again to go upstream. After this bear left at any other junctions.

The Land Rover track takes you deeper and deeper into the forest. There is a fine sense of remoteness to it, and you get occasional views of the Silver Flowe, now a nature reserve. After a while you pass a clearing with the Backhill of Bush bothy. This is reasonably comfortable as bothies go, with two wood-burning stoves.

After the bothy there is a gradual climb. A couple of miles after this you need to look out for a small stone cairn which marks the point where you leave the Land Rover track.

Turn left at the cairn and walk down the fire break for 300 metres. After this turn right and follow a faint track leading north. If it's not too wet you may be able to bike it. After a little way you cross a burn at a stone ledge, and after just over a mile you join another Land Rover track, where you turn right.

Note: in the opposite direction, leave the Land Rover track just before a metal bridge; the path is by a small bird cherry tree surrounded by lots of Sitka spruce.

After a mile or so Loch Doon comes into view. Turn left over a bridge to continue north, and turn left again at the next junction, unless you want to turn right to visit the café and craft shop (bike hire) or visit Loch Doon Castle (a re-erected ruin).

Loch Doon to Witches Bridge
(13 miles)

The next section is marked with red mountain-biking markers; you should follow these. The first section is part of a forest drive and there may be the odd car. There are views of the lochs together with some ups and downs, but overall it is a gentle climb.

You cross a public road soon after Loch Bradan to continue west, still following the red markers. When you meet the next public road, join it turning left (south). The red markers continue east after this, along another forest road to the village of Barr.

Witches Bridge to Glen Trool
(11 miles)

This section begins with a steep climb but after this it is predominately downhill, so it should be reasonably fast. Three miles before Glentrool Village turn left at the green and blue mountain-biking marker posts that signal the final part of the route. Follow the markers through the forest to the visitor centre.

TWEED VALLEY FORESTS

The forests of the Tweed Valley offer interesting mountain-biking, together with good views. They are located on steep-sided hills rising to over 500 metres, so there is always a climb to start with. There are four forest areas: Cardrona and Yair Hill, which are relatively small; Glentress, which has a bike-hire centre; and Elibank and Traquair Forest, which is the largest.

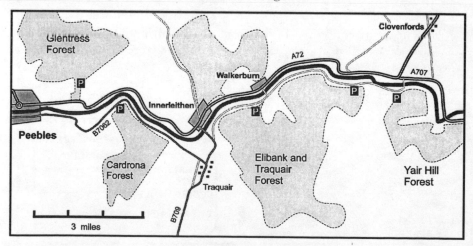

GLENTRESS FOREST

Hilly mountain-biking in the Tweed Valley.

GLENTRESS FOREST
ANDERSON TRAIL
(3 miles)
(Red markers; all forest roads)

Continue uphill on the main path, past the car parks and a carved wood red squirrel. Pass two ponds on the right, then shortly after some bird boxes nailed to tree trunks turn right down a rough track. Cross Glentress Burn, then turn left on to a forest road. Just after, by a picnic table, turn right to continue uphill.

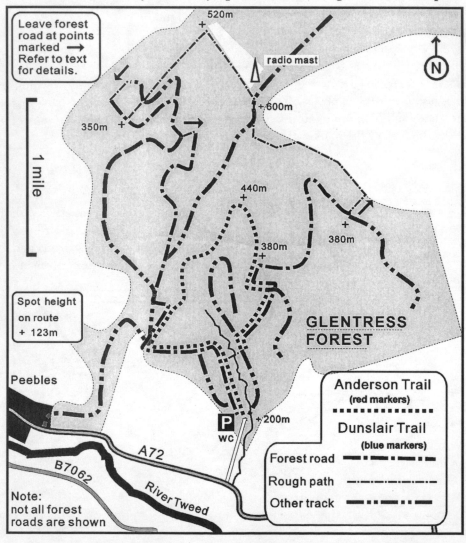

Leave forest road at points marked → Refer to text for details.

520m

radio mast

N

+600m

350m +

1 mile

440m
+

380m
+

380m
+

Spot height on route
+ 123m

GLENTRESS
FOREST

Peebles

Anderson Trail
(red markers)

Dunslair Trail
(blue markers)

P
WC

+200m

A72

B7062

River Tweed

Forest road

Rough path

Other track

Note:
not all forest
roads are shown

Turn left by a bench on to Anderson Road. The trail continues uphill for a little way to the point where the red and blue routes diverge.

For the Anderson Trail, continue straight uphill following red markers. The route curves round to the west, levels off, then descends steadily with fine views. Towards the end of the descent look out for marker posts indicating a left turn. Turn here to rejoin the blue route. Bear right at the next junction, then left at the next, to return to the start.

GLENTRESS FOREST
DUNSLAIR TRAIL
(11 miles)
(Blue markers; difficult)

This is the same as the Anderson Trail at first. Follow the instructions in the first paragraph, then turn right to follow blue markers. This track climbs gently at first, then descends gradually as it sweeps round the hill, all the time with good views. After just over a mile, look out for a blue marker post in a wider section and turn left up a steep path, leaving the forest road.

When you meet a dyke at the edge of the forest, turn left again to climb uphill very steeply towards a radio mast. You will have to push your bike at first. Just before the radio mast turn right on to a forest road, then at the mast bear left down a track at the forest edge. This descends gently at first, then turns south-west, descending steeply, with a great view.

Descend to a forest road and turn right. Follow this for a short distance, then turn left down a steep track (walk!). At the bottom turn left.

After a mile, at a sharp right-hand bend, turn left on to a rough track. This climbs steeply, then joins the end of another newer forest road. Follow this for just over a mile; after this keep straight on at the next junction, then turn left at a T-junction. Shortly after this you will see a gravel pit on the left; very soon after this turn right, dropping to a narrow track and joining the red route. Bear right at the next junction, then left at the next, to return to the start.

CARDRONA FOREST

CARDRONA FOREST
WALLACE'S HILL TRAIL
(8 miles)
(Green markers; difficult)

Both trails begin at the car park, just off the B7062. Cycle past a vehicle barrier, climbing steadily up the main track to the point where the two routes divide.

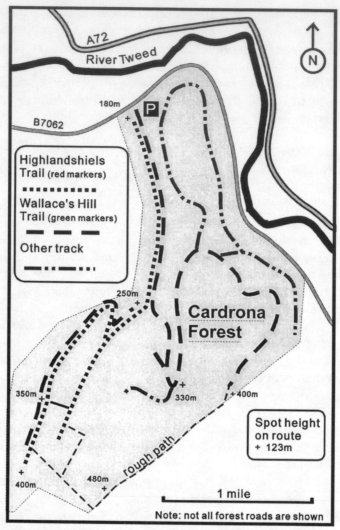

Continue straight on for the green route; turn right on to Glenpeggy Burn Road for the red.

The green route continues more steeply up the hill to another junction. Turn left here. The climb eases off, then there is a descent. Turn right at the next fork (Castleknowe South Road), and start climbing again. Bear right at the next junction to continue uphill on Wallace's Hill Road. There is a fine view looking down the River Tweed over Innerleithen, then the climb continues to the edge of the forest.

At the top of the hill bear left to go along the edge of the forest. There are open views to the left as the path skirts the edge of the trees. There is an occasional steep section, but most is bikeable. After just over a mile the path turns right and drops steeply to re-enter the forest. You can return on either leg of the Highlandshiels Trail.

Either continue straight down to cross the burn and climb briefly to join a forest road, or bear right on to a rough path 100 metres before the burn. If doing the latter, look for a steep little track in trees on the left-hand side and join this to get to the forest road which forms the Highlandshiels west leg. After this it's a straightforward descent all the way to the car park.

HIGHLANDSHIELS TRAIL

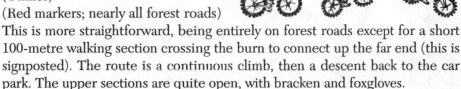

(4 miles)
(Red markers; nearly all forest roads)
This is more straightforward, being entirely on forest roads except for a short 100-metre walking section crossing the burn to connect up the far end (this is signposted). The route is a continuous climb, then a descent back to the car park. The upper sections are quite open, with bracken and foxgloves.

TRAQUAIR TO YAIR HILL

Two interesting bike routes in the Tweed Valley Forests.

THE MINCH MOOR TRAIL

(12 miles)
The Minch Moor Trail starts from the minor road on the south bank of the River Tweed, just west of the bridge crossing the river at Walkerburn; it is signed Elibank and Traquair Forest.

The route begins as a wide forest road, and mountain-bike signposts are quite infrequent. There is a steady climb through Sitka spruce, then a gentle descent to open country with birch trees and a view of Innerleithen. Turn right at the first T-junction. There are good views of the River Tweed through gaps in the trees, followed by a fast descent.

At the bottom, bear left at a junction to climb again, the village of Traquair below on the right. You cross the Southern Upland Way (thistle emblem), then there is another descent to a sharp bend; keep left here.

Following this there is another rise, another descent, then a short climb to a wide area for forestry vehicles to turn. Turn left at the bike-route sign, leaving the forest road. On this section you may need to get off and push. After a short way there is another bike signpost where you turn left, climbing steeply. This is definitely for walking, but after 25 metres bear right (at a sign), and you will be able to ride again.

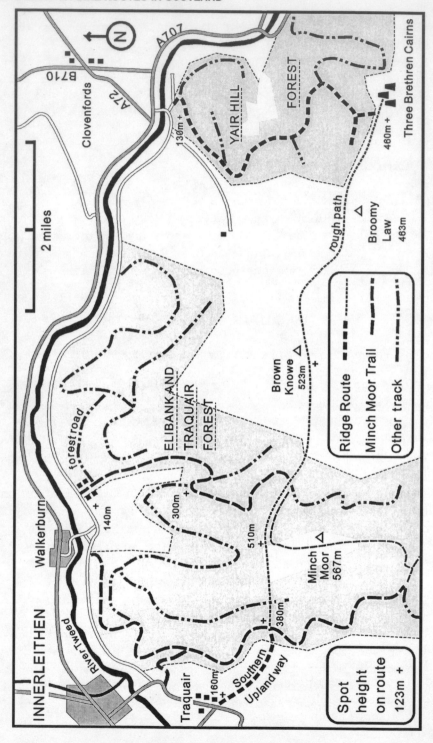

INNERLEITHEN

Walkerburn

Clovenfords

A707

B710

A72

River Tweed

Traquair

160m +

Southern
Upland way

Forest road

ELIBANK AND
TRAQUAIR
FOREST

YAIR HILL

FOREST

Three Brethren Cairns

460m +

rough path

Broomy
Law
463m

Brown
Knowe
523m

Minch
Moor
567m

510m +

380m

140m +

300m

130m +

2 miles

Ridge Route

Minch Moor Trail

Other track

Spot
height
on route
123m +

After this the path follows a dyke north through the forest, to the summit of Minch Moor. The top of the hill is visible some way off. At the top the panorama of the rolling Borders hills is visible all round. The three bumps to the east are the Eildon Hills.

Following this there is another fast descent to rejoin the Southern Upland Way. Turn right (east) here, to follow the ridge route until you meet a forest road. At this point turn left (north) to zoom down the hill again towards the River Tweed. Turn right at the first junction halfway down the hill, turn left at the next, then keep left by Bold Burn to rejoin the public road at four wooden forestry houses.

To return to your starting point, turn left up the minor road. To do the route in the reverse direction, you of course start at the four wooden houses.

RIDGE ROUTE TO YAIR HILL FOREST
(12 miles)

This starts in the village of Traquair. At the crossroads in the village take the cul-de-sac heading south-east following a Southern Upland Way sign. After 150 metres the road becomes a gravel track and climbs steeply. Shortly afterwards it becomes a simple track.

Climb to the first gate, cross a field and enter the forest. Continue up, cross a forest road (the other route), then climb steeply through dense trees. Cross a small burn and then another forest road, the climb becoming less steep and then leaving the forest in heather near the top of the hill.

After this you will pass the Cheese Well, so called because drovers used to drop crumbs of cheese into it in the hope of favours from the fairies who were said to haunt it. Soon after, you pass the summit of Minch Moor on your right. About here the path becomes smoother, flattening out. It then starts a long descent before climbing again to Hare Law. Watch for ruts in the track which can catch your wheel. At the bottom there is another forest road which you cross to continue along the ridgeway.

Continue east along this old drove road, crossing Hare Law. There is a right fork (Minchmoor Road) which you should ignore; bear left here to keep on high ground. After this the route crosses Brown Knowe, its highest point. Here the Eildon Hills near Melrose come into view. The first 100 metres after the Brown Knowe summit used to be a bit boggy, but there is a proper path now. After this there is a fast, tricky descent of about a mile.

At the bottom there is a sign telling you that this is not the turn-off for Broadmeadows Youth Hostel, which is a mile and a half further on. In any case keep straight on, climbing again with trees on the right, going round the north side of Broomy Law on a wide path. The village of Clovenfords can be seen on the left.

Soon you will encounter the sign telling you to turn right (south) for the youth hostel. Just ahead is Yair Hill Forest. Keep along the high track towards the Three Brethren cairns.

The return route is a left turn into the forest about 200 metres before you get to the Three Brethren cairns. It's worth going along to the cairns because there's a great view from the top of the hill.

To return to the public road, turn north into Yair Hill Forest 200 metres west of the Three Brethren cairns. This track drops steeply to another forest road, where you turn right. Descend again to another T-junction and turn left (turning right at this junction will eventually lead you to the A707 just north of Selkirk).

After this, keep on the main track and ignore all turn-offs. There is an initial descent, a slight rise, then a final descent to the edge of the forest near the River Tweed. When you get to the bottom of the second hill turn left at a T-junction to leave the forest. You meet the minor road on the south bank of the river near Ashiestiel Bridge. Return to Traquair is a left turn along the minor road; some of it could be done on forest tracks (see map).

If you are starting from Yair Hill Forest, note that the entry to the forest is via a dirt track immediately after the stone Ashiestiel Bridge and not through the Yair Camp Site entry, which is walking access only.

ROUTES NEAR EDINBURGH

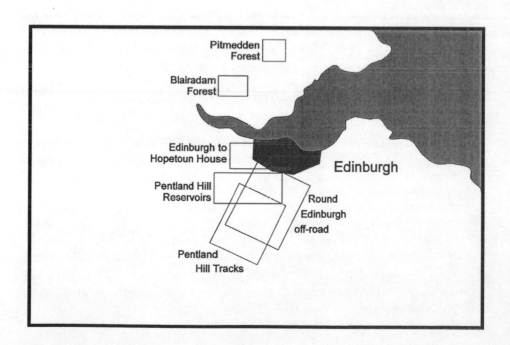

OVERVIEW

Edinburgh is lucky in that, unlike many other cities, it has wild land right next to the city boundary and even inside the city itself. Wild land, unlike well-groomed city parks, has mountain-biking possibilities. The Pentland Hills in particular are crossed by a number of rough tracks and rights of way, but there are quite a lot of biking possibilities apart from this.

Another advantage of Edinburgh is that it has a good network of bike paths: converted railway lines and canal towpaths. These have been built after pressure over the years by the local bike campaigning group (Spokes, the Lothian Cycle Campaign) and are now quite extensive. They aren't mountain-bike routes in themselves, but they are very handy for linking the off-road bits together.

Some of the routes make extensive use of canal towpaths etc., but then mountain-bike routes don't necessarily have to be on mountains! This especially applies to the route to Hopetoun House, and means that this route in particular is fairly flat. It still means you'll be getting dirt on your tyres, though, and it's a great little route taking you out of the city centre.

These factors mean that if you live in Edinburgh, or even if you are just visiting, you don't need to hop in a car to get to a mountain-bike route – it's right there next to you. In fact, traffic conditions being the way they are, it's probably quicker to get there on your bike. Not all the routes in this section are right next to Edinburgh; there are a couple near Fife which will benefit residents of Kinross and Kirkcaldy.

I live in Edinburgh. My kitchen window looks out on a car wash. When I'm washing the dishes I'm usually looking at some mountain-biker or other hosing the mud off his machine. Moral: dishes are boring – spend more time washing your bike!

ROUND EDINBURGH OFF-ROAD

37 miles, 70 per cent off-road, lots of country scenery.

This route uses four former railway lines and a canal towpath, and it crosses the Pentland Hills. The first part, to Balerno, could be done on any bike; a mountain-bike would be best after this.

TOLLCROSS TO BALERNO
(8 miles)

From the King's Theatre, go up Gilmore Place (opposite); take the first right to Lower Gilmore Place (by a church) and go over Leamington Lift Bridge to the canal. After two miles you go over a high aqueduct. Soon after, cross a footbridge over the canal and Lanark Road.

Keep right, going along a disused railway line by the Water of Leith. You go

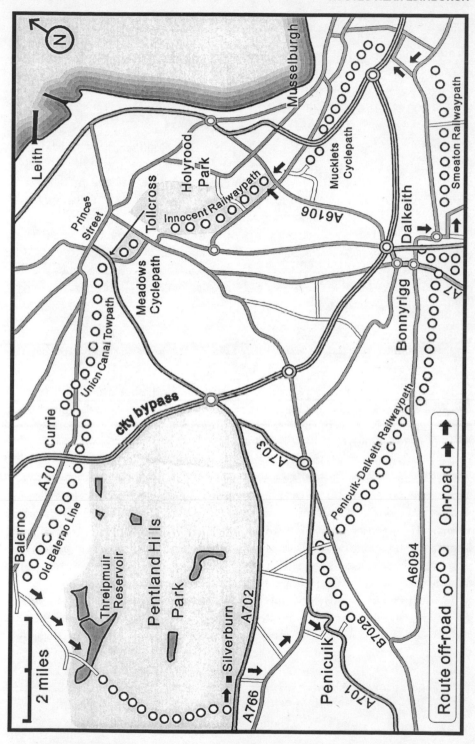

through a park, then a tunnel, then the route crosses access roads a couple of times. Continue in the same direction, looking for the dirt path on the other side. This section ends by Balerno High School in Bridge Road.

BALERNO TO PENICUIK
(9 miles)

Turn left on to Bridge Road, then left up Bavelaw Road, signposted Malleny House Garden (National Trust). Keep straight on up the hill to leave Balerno. At Red Moss Wildlife Reserve take the left fork towards the hills. Cross Threipmuir Reservoir, then at the T-junction at the top of Beech Avenue turn right, and then left (right-of-way sign).

After a climb, pass between West Kip on your left and Cap Law. Keep to the main path, dropping to Eastside Farm. There is a brief rise, then it drops again to the A702. Turn left here. If you cycle along the footpath by the road, watch out for boulders. At Silverburn turn right for Penicuik, then left on to the fairly quiet A766 towards the town.

PENICUIK TO DALKEITH
(8 miles)

In Penicuik, when you see playing fields and a 30mph sign, turn right (signposted Penicuik). At The Square, turn right by the Olympic Café, signposted Peebles. At the bottom of the hill, before the river, turn left down Valleyfield Road to the Penicuik to Dalkeith railway path.

There is a narrow section at Auchendinny, and then a tunnel. The path leaves the rail route to avoid a mining development. It is briefly broken by a road junction at Rosewell – cross over and you will see it again. After this it passes under the A6094 and ends at Bonnyrigg. Keep straight on. Cross Campview Road and go down by a swing park and a station platform with flower beds. Cross Dundas Street and go down Waverley Court (new houses) to a cycle path. You pass over a bypass road and end in a yard. Turn right down a dirt track, then left to another cycle path. Keep straight on to a station platform.

The surfaced path ends here and the next section may be muddy. Either carry on, passing under two bridges, or filter up a ramp to the right to the old Eskbank station yard. Bike through this, cross Lasswade Road by a shop and go through the garage forecourt opposite Melville Road. Turn left here, then, after passing the telephone exchange, turn right through a gate to meet the rail line again.

Whichever way, you'll meet another cycle path. Turn left and cross the River Esk on the Glen Esk Viaduct. This was built in 1847 and has recently been restored. Immediately after the viaduct, leave the cycle path. Turn right up steps by an indicator board. At more steps, turn left through trees, go along a bit, then drop to a public road. Bear right and cycle down the side of the road on a footpath, but join it at the bridge.

Bear left past Bridgend Court and turn left at traffic lights at the junction of Edinburgh Road and Dalkeith High Street.

DALKEITH TO TOLLCROSS
(12 miles)

Follow the main road (signposted Whitecraig, Musselburgh), crossing the River South Esk, to a roundabout. Take the second exit (Thornybank). Turn left on to the B6414 (there is a bike sign) and turn left to the Smeaton cycle path. This is tarmac at first, but becomes a dirt surface shortly before it ends at Whitecraig.

At the public road turn left, following the bike sign for Musselburgh. After a quarter-mile turn right down Cowpits Road (sign: River Esk Walkway 2.5). At the next bend leave the road (sign: River Esk Walkway 2). Go under the bypass and after a little way cross the river on a metal footbridge. Pass under a rail line to a mini-roundabout; go straight over into a cul-de-sac (new houses).

In the cul-de-sac turn left, right, then left again and go under the railway. Keep right and go under another rail line (*not under the bypass*) to emerge at Musselburgh Station. Turn left here to pass through the cycle-path barrier to Mucklets Path. Turn left under the city bypass, signposted Niddrie, then keep right to emerge at Newcraighall by a church building. Turn left here, then right at traffic lights to Duddingston Park South. Pass under a rail bridge. (Avoid the traffic lights by going right into Peacocktail Close, crossing the grass to Cleekim Drive and turning right at Duddingston Inn.)

Just after a roundabout, turn left to the Innocent Cycle Path. Follow this, crossing Duddingston Road, then cycle through the tunnel. End here, or to return to the start turn right through the housing estate and follow the red-brick path to The Engine Shed Café. Turn left to St Leonard's Lane, go down Rankeillor Street, cross Clerk Street and go down a path to Gifford Street. Turn left, then right through bollards to The Meadows cycle path leading to Tollcross and the King's Theatre.

PENTLAND HILL TRACKS

Challenging biking – just half an hour from the city.

There is a lot of pressure on these hills, walkers and mountain-bikers using them in large numbers. Be considerate and stop to let walkers pass. Keep to the rights of way. The Pentlands can seem as remote and as beautiful as any of Scotland's hills. Try to keep them that way – avoid fierce braking on wet grass. Tell someone where you're going, and wear a helmet.

ROUTE A
(4 miles)
**Eight Mile Burn
to Threipmuir Reservoir**

At the south end, the route starts 1.3 miles north-east of the junction of the A702 and A766, west of Penicuik (sign: Public Path to Balerno; also: Eastside Farm). At the north end, start at the bridge over Threipmuir Reservoir, as indicated on the map. Turn right at the top of Beech Avenue after the reservoir, then left before the private sign. There is a spur leading to Nine Mile Burn just south of the path summit.

ROUTE B
(2.5 miles + 3.5 on road)
Threipmuir Reservoir to Flotterstone

At the south end, start at Flotterstone Inn off the A702 north of Penicuik. The visitor centre is across the road from the inn. At the north end, start at Threipmuir as in route A, but turn left instead of right at the top of Beech Avenue. There are two high stiles. It is possible to get from Flotterstone to Eight Mile Burn by cycling on the footpath by the side of the A702.

ROUTE C
(2 miles)
Loganlea Reservoir to A702

This is very steep and needs care, particularly in the wet. At the south end it is signposted Public Footpath to Colinton and Balerno. If you meet water here, go left into the field. The path leads over a meadow to a gate, by way of Charlie's Loup (lift your bike over). After this it is a track through heather which becomes progressively steeper. At the north end it starts at the west end of Loganlea Reservoir, and is signposted Old Kirk Road to Penicuik.

ROUTE D
(2.5 miles)
**Harlaw Reservoir to
Glencorse Reservoir**

At the north end this is best approached from the crossroads at Wester Kinleith (marked X on map). From Balerno, turn left off Bavelaw Road into Harlaw Road, go up to the crossroads, then turn right towards the hills. From the Glencorse end the route is signposted Public Footpath to Balerno, Colinton and Currie.

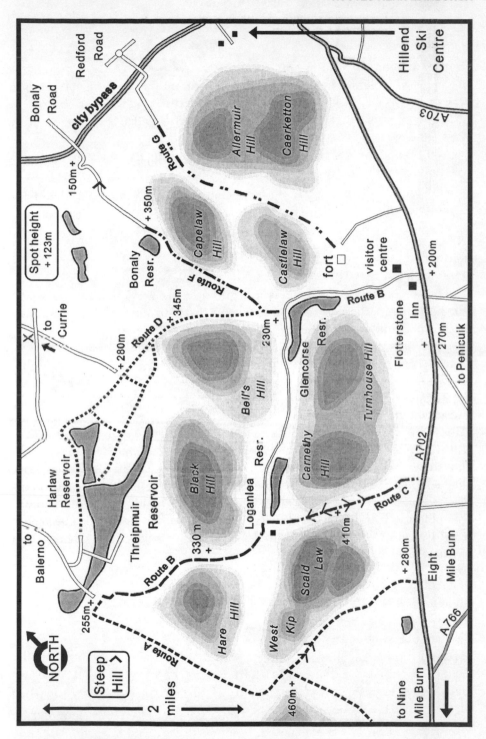

ROUTE F
(2.5 miles)

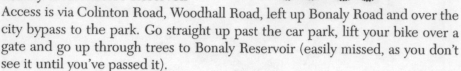

Bonaly to Glencorse Reservoir

Access is via Colinton Road, Woodhall Road, left up Bonaly Road and over the city bypass to the park. Go straight up past the car park, lift your bike over a gate and go up through trees to Bonaly Reservoir (easily missed, as you don't see it until you've passed it).

At a gate by the reservoir, turn right at the red military area sign. After this continue straight on, descending all the way to Glencorse. In the opposite direction start the same way as the Glencorse end of route D, but fork right for Colinton after a short climb.

ROUTE G
(2.5 miles)

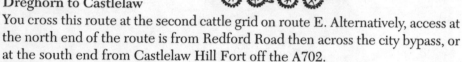

Dreghorn to Castlelaw

You cross this route at the second cattle grid on route E. Alternatively, access at the north end of the route is from Redford Road then across the city bypass, or at the south end from Castlelaw Hill Fort off the A702.

ROUTE H
(7 miles)

**West Linton to Harperrig
Reservoir via Cauldstane Slap**

This route is not on the map. Start on the A702 in West Linton. Go up Medwyn Road (signposted Baddinsgill) and keep straight on. The route becomes a track, and then a footpath. The summit of this old drove road is the Cauldstane Slap. The A70, leading to Balerno, is visible ahead (turn right for Balerno) and seems quite near, but the last mile before the reservoir is boggy and means you will have to carry your bike a lot. Wet feet are guaranteed if there has been recent rain! It is usually best to do the route as West Linton to Cauldstane Slap and return.

EDINBURGH TO HOPETOUN HOUSE

*23 miles – lots of canal
towpath and mostly flat!*

Start at the King's Theatre in Leven Street, near Tollcross. Go up Gilmore Place (opposite), then take the first right into Lower Gilmore Place (by a church). Pass over Leamington Lift Bridge and turn left on to the canal towpath. After two

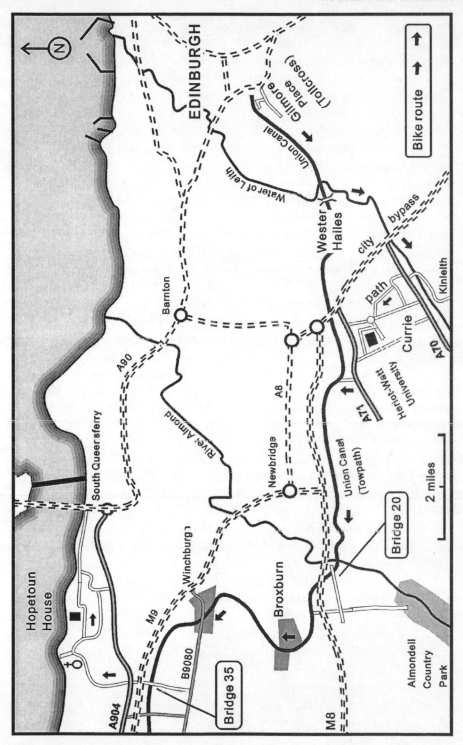

miles you pass over a high aqueduct leading over the Water of Leith. Shortly after this you will see a footbridge going over the canal. At the footbridge, leave the towpath and use the bridge to cross over the canal and Lanark Road.

Keep right to go along a disused railway line by the Water of Leith. Go through a tunnel, under a stone bridge, with Spylaw Public Park on the left. The route crosses access roads a couple of times; continue in the same direction, looking for the continuation of the dirt path on the other side. Go under the city bypass. *Note that the path continues to Balerno, but leave it a mile after the city bypass.*

Soon, on the left, you'll see a footbridge over the river; ignore it, but when you encounter asphalt again, pass between some large boulders. After 50 metres bear right by two large boulders on to the dirt path. Shortly after, cross the river to the left bank. Soon after this you meet an arched stone bridge. This is where we leave the river. Is this the right bridge? On the riverbank there will be steps leading down to the river, and on the left are more steps, curving up to the bridge.

Carry your bike up, turning left over the bridge, and cycle up to Lanark Road West. Turn right, then immediately left on to Muirwood Road (cycle-route sign: Riccarton, Heriot Watt). Muirwood Road turns left by some pylons.

Here is another bike sign: Riccarton, Heriot Watt, Wester Hailes. Go down the lane. Ignore the sign for Wester Hailes further on, keep straight on and cross the railway on a cyclist's level crossing. At the major road turn right, then left at the roundabout into Heriot Watt University.

After entering the university grounds, near a bus shelter, take the first right to Boundary Road East. Follow the road round as it curves to the west, passing over three road humps. When you see a yellow-painted vehicle barrier, continue straight on, cycling round it on to a potholed access road. Keep straight on to leave the university, then turn right on to the public road at the give-way signs.

This road joins the busy A71. Turn left here, signposted Kilmarnock. Carefully cross the main road and cycle along the far-side footpath until you come to Addiston Farm Road; go down this to meet the canal again. Continue west by crossing the bridge and turning left on to the canal towpath.

When the canal was built, the bridges over it were numbered; some numbers have been lost, as some bridges are gone. Note the number of each bridge as you go under it (the numbers are above each arch). Cross the River Almond on a high aqueduct, then, to get round the motorway (the canal is piped underneath), leave the canal at the first bridge (20), crossing it to continue west. The road runs parallel to a railway line for a mile, passing two right turn-offs before coming to a crossroads.

At the crossroads there is a left turn to Almondell Country Park – but you turn right. Go under a railway and the M8 motorway to meet the canal again.

Here at Learielaw Farm Road cross the bridge and join the towpath again for a traffic-free route through Broxburn.

As you leave Broxburn, the towpath is cut by the road. Cross this carefully and rejoin the towpath on the other side. After this carry on for 3.7 miles to bridge 35. This stone bridge has black iron railings, and the monogram 'HH' is carved in stone. Leave the canal, turning right (north) on to the road.

Continuing north, we go under another motorway, the M9, and then meet the A904. Cross over and go down the minor road by Abercorn Primary School, signposted Hopetoun House 2 miles. This great Adam mansion is open to the public from Easter to September (tel: 0131 331 2451). Turn left into Hopetoun House grounds to enter by the west gate.

Cycling through the grounds to South Queensferry is quite straightforward. It is reasonable to do this if you intend to visit the house or to be a customer of the garden centre, which is open all year. The garden centre has a tea room. If you want to visit the house itself you will have to pay an admission charge at a small kiosk which guards access.

Leave Hopetoun House by the main east gate and continue east by the shore road to South Queensferry, passing Port Edgar Water Sports Centre and ending up underneath the Forth Road Bridge.

Here you have a number of options: to cross the bridge to Fife, bike up to the bridge on the cycle path; to return to Edinburgh, go straight over underneath the bridge to Stewart Terrace and continue up the hill, turning right then left into Burgess Road (this leads to Station Road and the train station where you might be able to get on a train), or you could cycle back via Dalmeny and Barnton. Details of this, however, are in the road-cycling book.

PENTLAND HILL RESERVOIRS

An easy bike route with great scenery. Mostly on dirt tracks; distance 20 miles.

TOLLCROSS (EDINBURGH) TO BALERNO
(8 miles)

At Tollcross, start from the King's Theatre. Go up Gilmore Place (opposite), then take the first right to Lower Gilmore Place (by a church). Cross over Leamington Lift Bridge to the Union Canal towpath. Cycle along this for two miles. The towpath can be busy with pedestrians on Sunday afternoons, so making a start in the morning is a good idea. After two miles the towpath goes over a high aqueduct above the Water of Leith. Soon after this, leave the canal by crossing a footbridge over the canal and Lanark Road (A70).

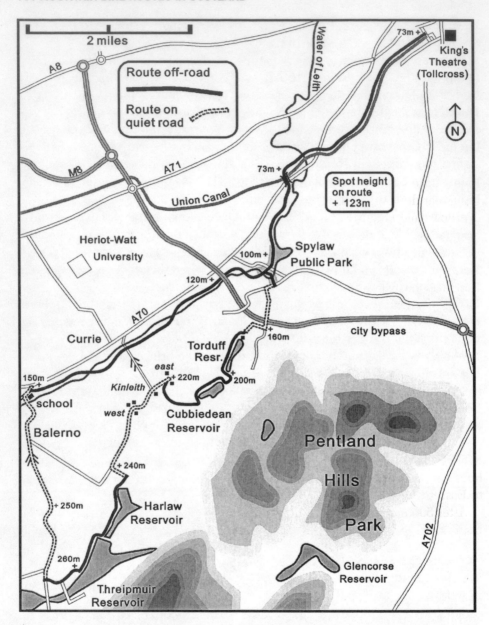

Keep right along a disused railway line by the Water of Leith; go through a tunnel leading to Spylaw Public Park and keep straight on. The route crosses access roads a couple of times; continue in the same direction, looking for the dirt path on the other side. This section ends in Balerno by the High School in Bridge Road.

BALERNO TO HARLAW RESERVOIR
(4 miles)

Turn left on to Bridge Road, then left up Bavelaw Road, signposted Malleny House Garden (National Trust). Keep straight on up the hill, climbing steadily, to leave Balerno. After just over a mile, at Red Moss Wildlife Reserve, take the left fork towards the hills.

After 400 metres turn left at Threipmuir car park and go down a rough track. Pass a locked gate (use the side gate), then bear right at the next gate, using the triangular detour. Continue along by the shore of Threipmuir Reservoir to the overflow sluiceway. If this is dry you can cycle along it; if not, use the little iron bridge.

Bear left after the sluice to continue along a straight track, with Harlaw Reservoir on the right. When you reach the dam at the far end of Harlaw Reservoir, cross it.

HARLAW RESERVOIR
TO TORDUFF RESERVOIR
(3 miles)

Leave Harlaw Reservoir by bearing left, past a red sandstone cottage. After 300 metres bear left on to the public road. When you see the sign 'Public Path to Glencorse', go in the opposite direction. Turn right at the next T-junction, by electricity pylons.

There is a slight descent with a view of the Forth Estuary, an S-bend at Wester Kinleith, then a gentle climb followed by a view of the city. Turn right at a white house, just before a steep descent to Currie, to continue in the same direction to Easter Kinleith.

After 500 metres you cross a burn on a stone bridge, then find yourself in a farm yard. Turn sharp right, reversing direction on to a rough track. This passes a Pentland Hills Park notice board, 'East Kinleith', then turns east again to Cubbiedean Reservoir.

Follow the main path past Cubbiedean Reservoir. This turns right at the far end by a cottage, then descends steeply to Torduff Reservoir. A footpath marked 'no bikes please' leads up towards Bonaly. Ignore this footpath and bear left to go round the west side of Torduff Reservoir.

TORDUFF RESERVOIR TO TOLLCROSS
(5 miles)

After Torduff there is a steep descent to Torduff Road. Turn left to cross over the city bypass. After this keep straight on down Bonaly Road, passing modern houses, and turn right at the T-junction at the foot on to Woodhall Road (opposite West Colinton House).

After 300 metres, turn left down a footpath. This is opposite a white house with black timbers. Walk down steps, then turn left down more steps just before the bridge carrying the public road. When you are on the same level as the Water of Leith, cross the river on a footbridge.

After crossing, a Water of Leith Walkway sign indicates you should turn right to return to the city. This, however, leads to footsteps. Avoid these by turning left past the big house with the monkey puzzle tree, then turning right towards the path.

Returning to Tollcross after this is on the same route you came out on. Keep to the former railway line track as far as the Union Canal, then turn right (east). Because of the layout of the bridge footpath, this right turn when you meet the canal is actually a double left turn. The end of the canal and Tollcross is two miles further north-east. At the end of the canal towpath, cross the lift bridge, then turn left down Lower Gilmore Place, then left to Gilmore Place to return to the King's Theatre.

PITMEDDEN FOREST

An attractive small forest near Kinross.

INTRODUCTION

Pitmedden Forest stands on steep-sided hills between Newburgh and Auchtermuchty.

PITMEDDEN FOREST

Pitmedden Forest forms a rough circle, broken to the south-east. Start at the car park on the west side. Climb up the hill and travel south on the forest road, taking the second left near the top of the hill.

Just after, at a right bend, there is an extra footpath loop (marked # on map); turn left through the woods to do this.

From the top of the hill there is a descent, with a view of the Lomond Hills. Just after a bend, you encounter a left turn followed by a crossroads. The first

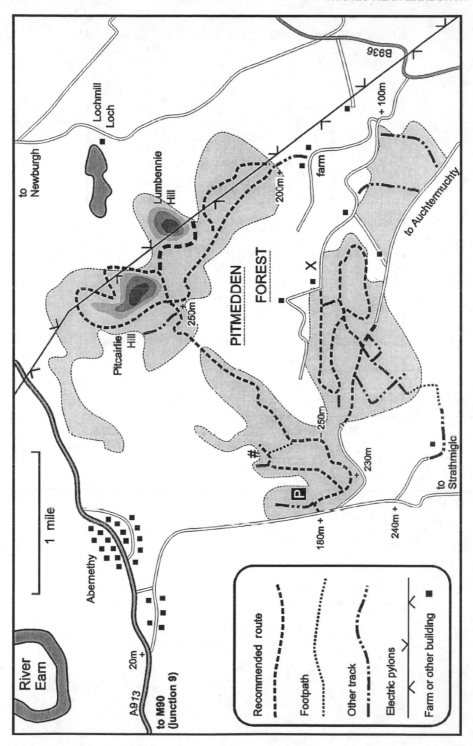

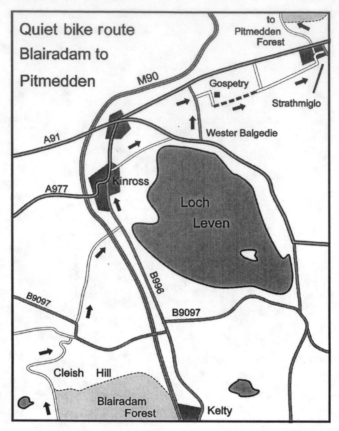

left is a dead end but the second left goes round Pitcairlie Hill. This gives a view over the River Tay.

Halfway round you meet an electricity line; try to follow the footpath under the pylons! Shortly after this there is another T-junction and you can turn left or right. Turning left takes you round Lumbennie Hill – great views, but the track ends under the pylons. The alternative is to turn right and keep in the forest.

For access to the forest from the road marked X on the map, keep on the road until you see a small bungalow with a pigeon loft and horses; then enter the forest where the road takes a sharp turn to the right up a hill.

BLAIRADAM FOREST

LOCATION
Blairadam Forest is west of Kelty, off junction 4 on the M90. It is less hilly than Pitmedden, but has lots of interesting trails meandering through mixed woodland.

BLAIRADAM FOREST

The best part of Blairadam Forest is the east side near Kelty. Here the forest is more open and you'll see lots of beech, birch and oak as well as the usual spruce.

The main forest tracks are fairly easy, but get away from these and there are lots of interesting bits joining up parts of the main tracks. Near the forest edge there are good views of the nearby hills.

West of the Cleish Hill road the forest is all spruce; Knockhill motorcycle racing circuit may be heard. Trails are more limited; the track to the south of Loch Glow offers a longer run; gates could be locked. Loch Glow may be busy with anglers.

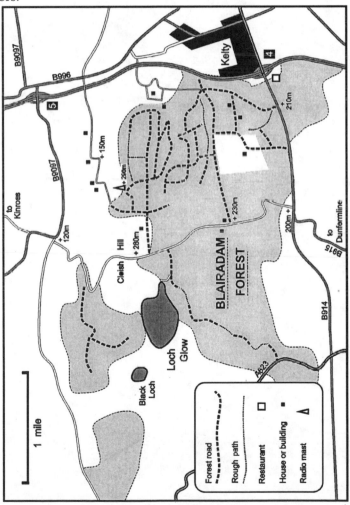

ROUTES NEAR GLASGOW

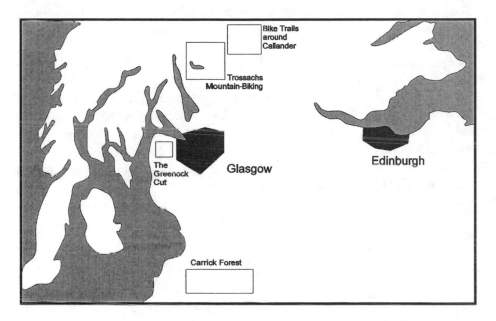

OVERVIEW

You have to go a bit further from the city centre in Glasgow to find a mountain-bike route, but when you do get there the quality is superb. I'm speaking, of course, about the Trossachs, which are only 20 miles from Glasgow and have an enormous variety of mountain-bike routes, and great scenery too.

There are other options as well; the routes around Loch Lubnaig and Loch Venachar are attractive and particularly suitable for children. Another possibility is the off-road tracks in the vicinity of the Greenock Cut; these are much nearer to Glasgow, and there's even a Sustrans cycle path to take you there from Glasgow city centre. This starts at the Scottish Exhibition and Conference Centre (SECC) in central Glasgow.

An interesting possibility near Ayr is Carrick Forest. This is described in the Southern Scotland chapter. There are many more routes 30 or so miles from Glasgow in the Loch Tay area; these are described under the Eastern Highlands.

THE GREENOCK CUT
and other tracks

An interesting day out, mostly easy hills, good views.

INTRODUCTION

Everyone in Greenock knows about the Greenock Cut; nobody anywhere else seems even to have heard of it.

My friend Dave, who had been brought up in Greenock, had been telling me about it for years. Eventually one day I cracked, and over we went to check it out.

Breakfast in the café in Greenock reminded me of my own childhood: the coffee came in a teapot; milk was compulsory.

The Greenock Cut is a sort of mini-canal, built to provide drinking water for the town and water power for its industry. It was finished in 1827, powering 19 water wheels and providing 21,000 cubic feet of water a day to the town. Naturally there's a path beside it, and that's what we bike along.

The views are pretty good, as you are 500 feet above the town and can see right over the Clyde to the Kyles of Bute. Once you've finished the Greenock Cut you can do the Kelly Cut, or explore miles of tracks and minor roads around the various reservoirs.

THE GREENOCK CUT
(5 miles)

Reaching The Cut from Greenock is mostly a matter of going up the steepest hill. From Greenock Central train station (trains take bikes) go uphill, turn right, then left – and keep going uphill.

Turn right at the sugar refinery, then left at the Old Largs Road sign. Follow a sign for The Cut, then turn left up a minor road (no sign). Do not go downhill at any time; if you get lost, ask anyone.

Water still flows in The Cut, but nobody is drinking it nowadays. As you can see from the map, water flowed from Loch Thom to Greenock in a clockwise direction.

Biking round anti-clockwise gives great views towards the Kyles of Bute but it will be slightly slower, as it's a gentle uphill. Going round clockwise can be quite fast and more technical, as the path is fairly narrow. The aqueduct cuts deeply into small gorges as it goes round the hill following its contour; these are wooded and quite pretty.

There are no particular hazards apart from a few gates not designed for bikes. The easiest way round these is on the aqueduct side. We met no pedestrians at

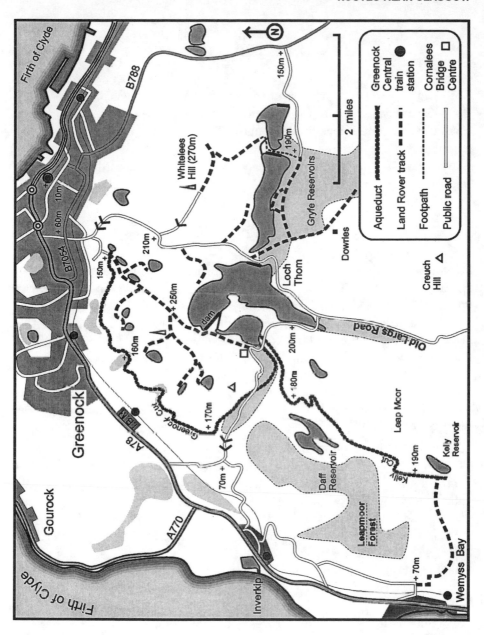

all except in the area of Cornalees Bridge Centre by Loch Thom, and they'd all got there by car.

It's necessary to leave The Cut briefly when crossing the minor road leading west from Loch Thom; apart from this there are no road crossings.

THE KELLY CUT
(4 miles)

The Kelly Cut is an extension of the Greenock Cut. It was built in 1845 to increase the water supply. Construction is similar to the Greenock Cut but the path is wider, if occasionally quite bumpy. The first 500 metres of the Kelly Cut forms part of a nature trail based at Cornalees Bridge Centre. The centre doesn't have a café, but it does have a tea and coffee machine, and the warden sells chocolate biscuits!

CIRCULAR ROUTES

If you are using the train you could return from a different station. One possibility would be to go out on the Greenock Cut, then take the Kelly Cut, then take the track down the hill towards Wemyss Bay.

Alternatively, return could be on the minor roads to the east of the A78, then via Loch Thom and Land Rover tracks to Greenock.

The minor road going round Loch Thom is very quiet; this could be made part of a Greenock Cut circuit leading to forest tracks to the south of the Gryfe Reservoirs. Return to Greenock on the B788.

Whitelees Hill is the highest point that can be reached on a bike; it's quite easy to reach via the Old Largs Road.

GREENOCK CUT HISTORY

The engineer who planned and built The Cut was Robert Thom. The purpose of the aqueduct was to carry water from the Great Reservoir, now named after him, to Greenock. It would provide water for the town and power for a paper mill, power looms, a sugar refinery and a bakery.

The excavation took 12 months to complete and included a compensation reservoir where the water was stored to regulate the flow. The water powered 19 water wheels, the largest of which was 70 feet in diameter, with 160 buckets. Each bucket contained 100 gallons of water, and it produced 200 horsepower.

The power unit most commonly quoted nowadays in connection with Greenock industry is the megabyte, Greenock being the home of IBM's PC manufacturing plant. Prior to this, Greenock produced ocean liners and dreadnought battleships.

Trossachs Mountain-Biking

Often hilly, but lots of choices; great scenery.

Introduction

Routes are marked with coloured posts. Loch Ard Forest is better for beginners than Achray Forest. Remember that there are other users of the forest: walkers and the timber industry. Show consideration to walkers; routes may have diversions due to logging operations.

Loch Ard Forest

(Green 15 miles; both reds 9 miles; both purples 4; blue 7)

The prettiest starting point in Loch Ard Forest is at Milton. This gives access to the flatter routes, including the easy purple one. Leave Aberfoyle going west, signposted Inversnaid Scenic Route. After a mile turn left in Milton, bearing left down the side of a cottage with a hooped steel fence to the forest car park. The red and purple trails are a right turn just before the car park. For the green, or to do the red clockwise, carry straight on.

The simplest thing is to follow the coloured markers. An easy ride would be to cycle the little purple loop by the loch for a picnic. A much longer ride (14 x 2 = 28 miles) is to the West Highland Way at Loch Lomond. The track runs by Duchray Water until it leaves the forest; follow the pylons. It then skirts round the north side of Ben Lomond. The West Highland Way is not bikeable at Loch Lomond.

The green route is technically interesting. Start at Milton, or follow the instructions here to join via the blue route. Leave Aberfoyle as before but turn left (south) at the crossroads at the west end of the village. After 200 metres, turn right by the Covenanters Inn to a forest road with an overhead phone line. The blue route loops off the main track, north and south round Lochan Spling. Do both loops, south last.

Turn left where the south loop rejoins the main track by a ruined cottage. Bear right at the next junction and follow little bridges with iron railings over the Castle Burn. Pass under an electricity line and an aqueduct, with a white cottage to the right. When you see a right turn over a bridge you can get to Aberfoyle on the red; for the green keep straight on.

Climb past Victorian water-board machinery. Eventually meet a concrete bridge. Turn left here, then left again to take the red route; bear right to keep on the green. Climb steeply, with views of Ben Venue behind; there is a view across the Forth Valley towards Stirling, then a fast descent, the Lake of Menteith far ahead. At the next junction, take either leg and drop down to the

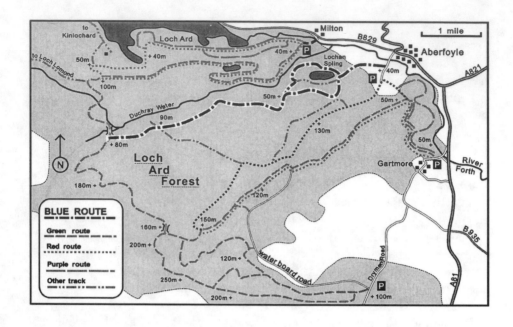

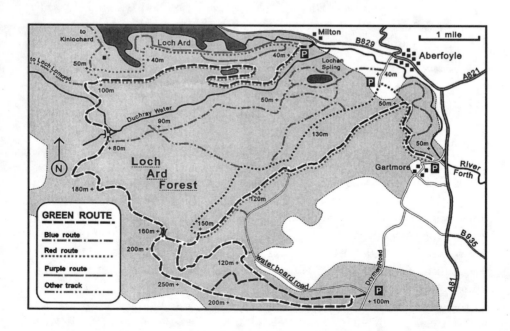

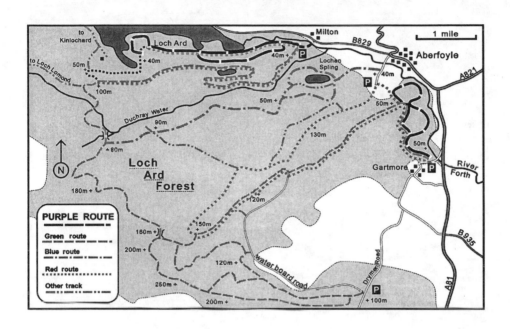

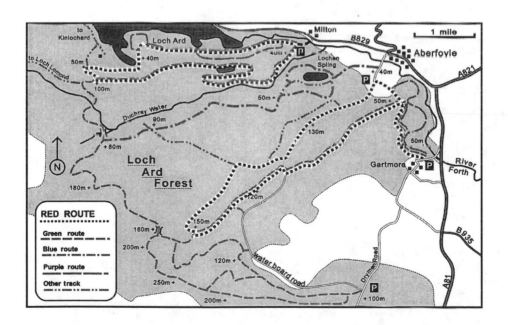

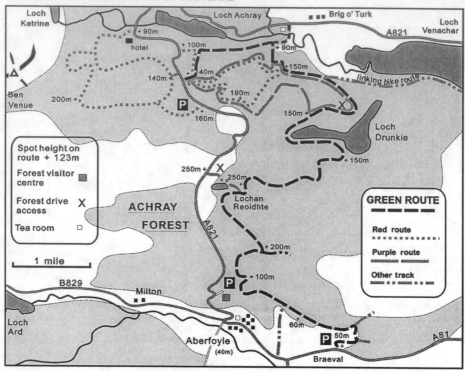

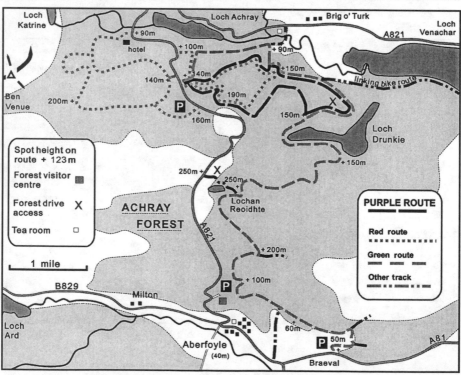

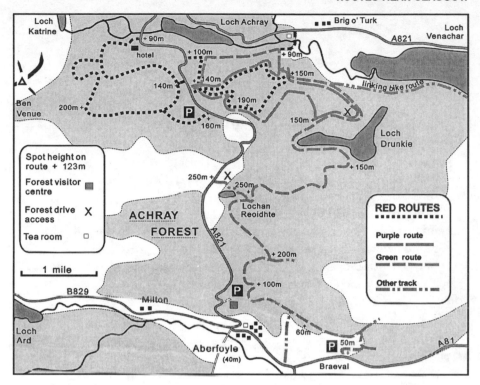

public road. Here there are two options: return on the green, using the opposite leg to the one you came down on, or use the water-board road. In the latter case you eventually meet the red route. You can return in either direction. The first part of the water-board road is surfaced.

ACHRAY FOREST

(Green 13.5 miles; western red 7 miles; others 3 or 4 miles)

Covering the hills either side of The Duke's Pass, Achray Forest has some long, steep gradients making for interesting biking. For the green, start just east of Aberfoyle, at the Braeval car park, on the A81. Alternatively, start at the Forest Visitor Centre off the A821. A long, steep climb takes you to the top of the pass, from where there is a fast descent to Loch Drunkie (where there are toilets).

The north end of the western red route starts behind the Loch Achray Hotel; for all the other routes refer to the map. Another bike trail leads along the south side of Loch Venachar towards Callander, which gives access to another set of bike trails. A useful finishing point just east of Loch Achray, on the A821, is the Byre restaurant. The best tea room in Aberfoyle is at the A821/B829 junction.

BIKE TRAILS AROUND CALLANDER

An easy route for families, with more difficult options.

INTRODUCTION

A former railway line, that of the Caledonian Railway Company, forms the backbone of this route. The railway path runs from Callander to Strathyre (9 miles).

It winds initially past the Falls of Leny, through birch and oak, then along the west side of Loch Lubnaig. The cycle path was constructed about ten years ago by Sustrans, the cycle-path charity.

Cycle paths along former railway lines have very easy gradients. The same cannot be said of the forest tracks on the slopes of Ben Ledi immediately above. These are marked as mountain-bike routes by the Forestry Commission.

There are other options too, including a quiet route along the south side of Loch Venachar which leads to mountain-bike trails in the Trossachs, and a very quiet road cycle round Loch Katrine.

CALLANDER TO STRATHYRE
(9 miles)

The main railway-path route starts in Callander, off the main road just west of the Dreadnought Hotel (car park and toilets). It sweeps to the south of the river, then crosses the A821 (children should take care). After this there are no more road crossings.

There is a long straight section leading to the Falls of Leny. Near here the old rail line was carried over the river, but the bridge is gone. The cycle-path builders elected to keep on the left bank, so the next section is more winding until it meets the old rail line again.

Keep straight on; cars are prevented from using the next section by a padlocked barrier. There is a tarmac surface here, but this soon runs out again at Forestry Commission chalets.

If you are intending to do the purple mountain-biking loop here, watch out for coloured marker posts indicating a left turn (see map). The higher trails offer good views towards Ben Vorlich on the other side of the loch but are steep.

There is an attractive picnic spot by the lochside, just beyond the chalets. The path runs by the loch in trees; there is a slight incline when you meet the second (red) mountain-biking loop.

Shortly after this you encounter a pile of china sinks; these have been here for at least 15 years to my knowledge and their origin is a mystery, but at least they serve as a marker for turning right (there is also a signpost).

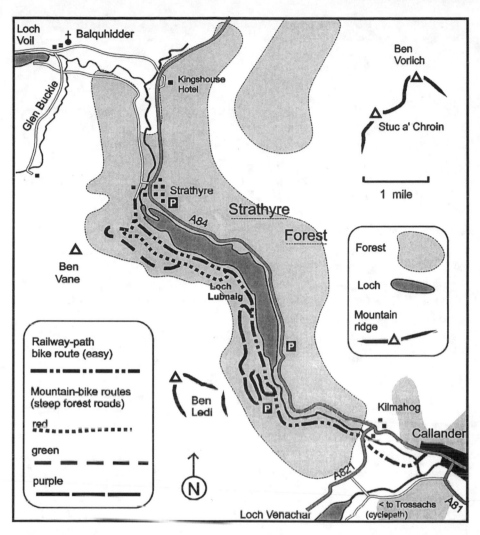

The last section at the end of the loch is on a footpath, a rise to meet a minor road. After this there is a drop through more trees. Turn right at the junction for Strathyre, which has a choice of pubs and tea rooms; there is also a village shop.

STRATHYRE TO BALQUHIDDER AND BEYOND

(4 miles to Balquhidder)

There is an option to continue northwards on the minor road to Balquhidder. This is very quiet but initially steep, climbing through trees.

The last section towards Loch Voil is flat. The little church at Balquhidder is the site of Rob Roy's grave. A fragment of poetry, on a wall in the graveyard, reminds you of your own mortality.

Love all you meet – no season know nor clime,
Nor, days, weeks, months – which are the rags of time.

After Balquhidder you could visit the Kingshouse Hotel two miles east of Balquhidder, which does bar lunches etc.

Please note it is impossible to travel directly between Strathyre Forest and Glen Buckie with a bike. The only route is via Balquhidder.

The track bed of the old rail line is still mostly intact north of Strathyre; hopefully one day this will also be a bike path. Currently it's broken just north of the Kingshouse at a sheep farm. The farmer is quite adamant that he doesn't want any mountain-bikers trying to find a way through.

It's possible to rejoin the rail line at the far side of Lochearnhead. A very steep footpath leads up to it, from near the former rail bridge by the scout station. From here you can mountain-bike most of the way up Glen Ogle.

Beyond Glen Ogle the line continues into Glen Dochart, meeting the A85 at a caravan site. This is private land; one of the bridges is missing; the way is barred by an electric fence.

LOCH VENACHAR

There is an interesting bike path on the south side of Loch Venachar; this connects to mountain-bike routes in Achray Forest in the Trossachs. To reach this, bike west along the minor road just off the A81 south of Callander (see map). Once you reach Loch Venachar, the cycle path is signposted.

TOURIST INFORMATION ETC.

Callander: 01877-30342; Killin Youth Hostel (just north of here): 01567-820546.

EASTERN HIGHLANDS

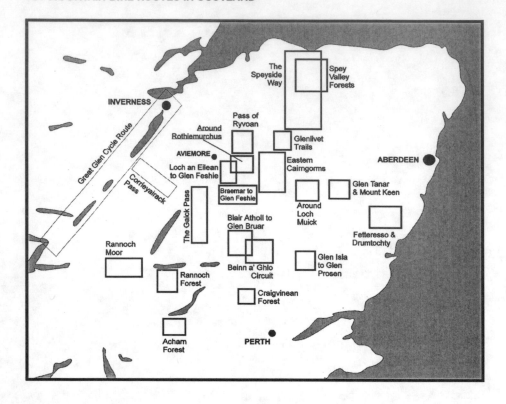

OVERVIEW

As you can see from the map, there are a lot of bike routes here and many are close together, which means you can link them up in all sorts of interesting ways. They vary quite a lot too. Because of this I'm giving them in tabular form, so that you can easily pick out the sort of thing you want. I hope this gives you some good ideas, whether it's for an afternoon out or a week-long trip!

GOOD FOR CHILDREN
Acharn Forest and Loch Tay
Craigvinean Forest
Around Rothiemurchus
Glenlivet Mountain-Bike Trails (part)
The Speyside Way (parts)
Spey Valley Forests
Around Loch Muick (part)
Glen Tanar and Mount Keen (part)
Fetteresso and Drumtochty

ROUTES TO LINK UP
(Given in sequence)
The Speyside Way
Spey Valley Forests
Glenlivet Mountain-Bike Trails
Eastern Cairngorms
Braemar to Glen Feshie
Loch an Eilean to Glen Feshie
Around Rothiemurchus
Pass of Ryvoan

LONGER, MORE DIFFICULT ROUTES

Across Rannoch Moor

Beinn a' Ghlo Circuit

Blair Atholl to Glen Bruar

The Gaick Pass

Pass of Ryvoan

Glen Isla to Glen Prosen

Braemar to Glen Feshie

Eastern Cairngorms

Glenlivet Mountain-Bike Trails (parts)

The Speyside Way (parts)

Around Loch Muick (part)

Glen Tanar and Mount Keen (part)

VERY SCENIC FOREST ROUTES

Acharn Forest and Loch Tay

Rannoch Forest

Around Rothiemurchus

Pass of Ryvoan (not all forest)

Loch an Eilean to Glen Feshie

Glen Tanar and Mount Keen (part)

ROUTES TO LINK UP

Loch an Eilean to Glen Feshie

The Gaick Pass

(then via A9 cycle path to)

Blair Atholl to Glen Bruar

Beinn a' Ghlo Circuit

Around Loch Muick

(route to Glen Clova,

then via back roads to)

Glen Isla to Glen Prosen

NOTES

It's also possible to connect to routes in the Northern and Western Highlands.

Some of the linking routes are difficult with long days in remote terrain.

The fact that a route is good for children doesn't mean it's boring for experts!

ACHARN FOREST AND LOCH TAY

Forest trails – great views of Loch Tay and Ben Lawers.

INTRODUCTION

Acharn Forest isn't anything special as far as the actual biking goes, being mostly forest roads. The forest itself is pretty standard too, with uniform Sitka spruce. What's so good about it, then? Answer: the views.

Biking east, the views consist of the Ben Lawers range and Loch Tay. These are some of the most scenic mountains in the southern highlands and run from the Tarmachan Ridge at the west end, through Ben Lawers itself in the centre, to Meall Garbh in the east.

Biking west the views are equally good, looking over the lush Breadalbane valley towards Ben Heasgarnich.

The routes are not signposted as mountain-bike routes but there is a sign welcoming walkers. There is a mountain-bike hire shop in Killin that sends their customers to this area.

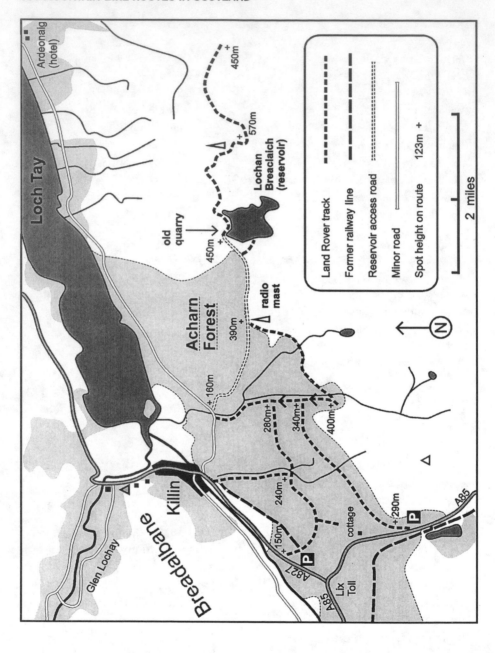

HIGH-LEVEL ROUTE

Being high up, this offers the best views of all, and if you are driving to the start the logical place to begin is the high-level car park just off the A85.

This is just over a mile south of the Lix Toll junction or, if you're coming from the south, at the top of Glen Ogle just north of Lochearnhead. In summer there is usually a man in a trailer in the car park selling hot snacks.

Bike through the car park and under a barrier intended to prevent high vehicles gaining entry to the trail. After a short distance you pass a memorial to an RAF pilot and shortly after this you meet a locked gate.

Pass through the gate using the side gate; there is a gentle climb and Ben Lawers and Loch Tay come into view. After a couple of miles you descend to a T-junction.

Turning left here will take you rapidly to the lower-level trails. To continue at high level turn right and climb steeply up beside the burn. After a short distance the forest road resumes its eastward direction and levels off. You pass a water pipe, meet another gate, then descend to meet the access road for the Lochan Breaclaich reservoir.

You have three choices here: to descend to the south Loch Tay road and return on that; to return on the lower-level forest trails by descending the same way; or to climb to Lochan Breaclaich and possibly beyond.

LOWER-LEVEL TRAILS

Access to these is from a small car park north-east of the Lix Toll junction on the A827; or from just outside Killin; or from the south Loch Tay road.

From all over the forest you get fine views over Breadalbane. The views of Ben Lawers aren't so good as higher up, and Loch Tay is only occasionally visible, but the forest is more varied with small areas of natural woodland appearing amongst the plantation spruce.

Starting at the east end of the forest, particularly from the south Loch Tay road, involves more of a climb. If you want to avoid biking up serious hills it's best to go round the circuit in an anti-clockwise direction, as the hills this way are more gentle.

LOCHAN BREACLAICH AND BEYOND

The access road to the reservoir is tarmac as far as the dam; thereafter it becomes a Land Rover track. This whole section is very hilly, with lots of steep climbs and descents, and isn't really suitable for young children.

The track ends about two miles south of Ardeonaig on Loch Tay. A rough footpath leads down to the public road at Ardeonaig but the farmer objects to mountain-bikers using it; this is why it isn't shown on the map. Return the way you came.

It is possible, if you don't mind walking over rough ground for just over a mile, to connect the end of this trail to Land Rover tracks in Glen Lednock. This gives access to more off-road biking around Ben Chonzie. You eventually come out near Comrie, just east of Loch Earn.

OTHER INFORMATION

The road up Glen Lochay (see map) is very quiet and pretty; after going along this for seven miles you can either climb steeply on a Hydro Board road into Glen Lyon or explore more Land Rover tracks on the south side of Ben Heasgarnich.

Mountain-bike hire from:
Killin Outdoor Centre
Main Street
Killin FK21 8UJ
Tel 01567-820652

RANNOCH FOREST

Interesting mountain-biking in dramatic scenery.

This is one of the most beautiful areas of Scotland and the routes reflect it, with fine views of the hills, and woods of Scots pine, birch and Sitka spruce on the lower sections. Two routes are described; neither is signposted. The first route is entirely in Rannoch Forest, except for a road section to return to the start. The other takes you south over the hills to Glen Lyon.

CARIE TO BRIDGE OF GAUR

(22 miles circular)
Start near the car park and picnic site at Carie, three miles west of Kinloch Rannoch, on the south shore of Loch Rannoch. There is a sign at the car park:

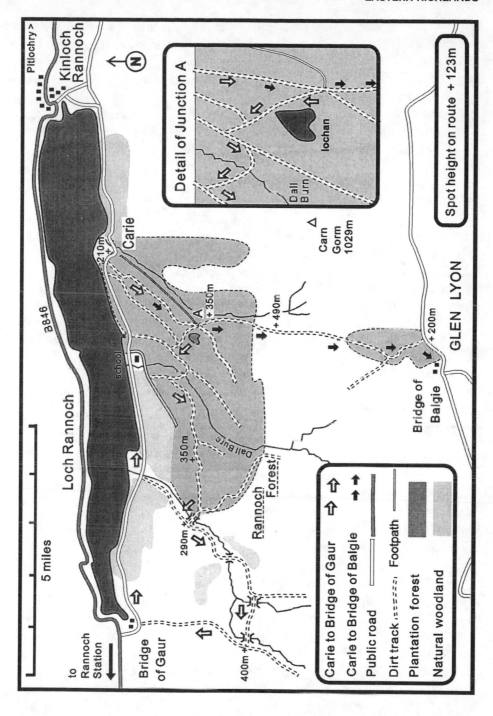

Detail of Junction A

lochan

Dall Burn

Spot height on route + 123m

Carn Gorm 1029m

Pitlochry >

Kinloch Rannoch

N

Carie

+ 210m

+ 350m

A

+ 490m

B846

Loch Rannoch

school

+ 200m

GLEN LYON

Bridge of Balgie

5 miles

350m +

Dall Burn

Rannoch Forest

290m +

to Rannoch Station

Bridge of Gaur

400m +

Carie to Bridge of Gaur

Carie to Bridge of Balgie

Public road

Dirt track ::::::::::: Footpath

Plantation forest

Natural woodland

87

'Public Path to Glen Lyon'. Mountain-bikers used to use this first footpath section but this is quite narrow so they are now directed to use the forest road just west of it. This runs parallel to the footpath and begins just west of the car park (see map). Continue south along the forest road for two miles until you come to a crossroads (see map insert).

At the crossroads turn right to go north. (The other route continues south.) The track leading south-west is a dead end. After a short distance you pass a lochan on the left, then bear left on to a wide forest road. Continue downhill, ignoring a track that joins from the right but turning sharp left at the next T-junction. A little way after this, at the next junction, bear right to cross the Dall Burn. After the bridge, climb uphill to a T-junction and turn left.

The track goes upstream on the north bank of the burn and gradually curves round to the west. The forest becomes more open, giving good views of the hills to the south. At a left bend the track turns north, becoming a new forest road; bear right here to continue west along the older path. Two miles later you drop to another burn and leave the forest. Cross the bridge, then turn left (south).

The path winds south, then west, between two hills with lots of natural Scots pine; two tracks lead south towards the hill of Garbh Mheall, and these could be explored. Otherwise continue west, crossing three bridges. At the last bridge turn right (north), and descend steeply to Bridge of Gaur on the south side of Loch Rannoch. There is a shop just west of here which has food, drinks, scones, ice cream, etc. Return to the start by cycling east on the south Loch Rannoch road.

CARIE TO BRIDGE OF BALGIE
(8 miles)

This is the same as the first route as far as the forest junction, but here you continue south. There is a locked gate and a deer fence where you leave the forest and it is necessary to carry your bike over this, using the two-metre-high ladder provided for walkers.

On leaving the forest the biking becomes more difficult for several hundred metres, but after crossing a burn this is no longer the case. Here you catch your first sight of the Ben Lawers range ahead. The path passes an old iron fence at its summit, then drops to a wooden bridge. Following this there is a flat section, with the Allt Ghallabhaich burn plunging steeply to your right. You enter forest again after crossing above a waterfall; remember to shut the gate.

The summit of Ben Lawers can briefly be seen ahead before the path plunges steeply into trees. There is another gate, also not locked, and then an easier gradient. Shortly after, you pass a new plantation on your left, then finally descend more gently to another gate, where you meet the public road.

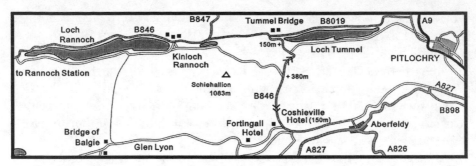

The post office at Bridge of Balgie, one mile west, can provide tea, coffee and home baking and also sells drinks and chocolate etc. Otherwise the nearest refreshment stop is the Fortingall Hotel ten miles down Glen Lyon (see map). An attractive option here in the summer is cream teas on the lawn; there are also hotels or tea rooms at Coshieville, Tummel Bridge and Kinloch Rannoch.

You can return by biking down Glen Lyon, then over the shoulder of Schiehallion to Kinloch Rannoch (26 miles, see map). If you are doing the route in a northerly direction, start east of Bridge of Balgie, by the church and war memorial.

ACROSS RANNOCH MOOR

This is not easy, but it could be a very useful link to join Cairngorm routes to the west of Scotland.

INTRODUCTION

I'd known for years there was a route of sorts across Rannoch Moor; the question was: could you bike it?

The problem became more interesting last year when Michael from Tubingen in Germany hired me and my BikeBus to carry the luggage for a party of 24 cyclists from Rannoch Station to the Kingshouse Hotel. They were clearly going to do it. Could I let a group of foreigners show me how it was done? Well, obviously, yes – after all, they were paying me to drive over 100 miles by Loch Tay to get there. They only had 13 miles to do.

Fortunately it was dry weather when I met Michael in Aberfeldy to pick up the luggage. I saw them off at Rannoch Station; the party included two grannies over 65 and several children. The bus and the cyclists arrived at the Kingshouse Hotel at about the same time.

Oh well, I was just going to have to do it then. The next opportunity was when I had a party of Spokes cyclists from Edinburgh cycling round Loch Rannoch. Dave and I, together with a guy from Spain who didn't fancy road cycling, shot off to try it out. Unfortunately it had been raining solidly for a week. As far as I am concerned, for it to be a bike route I have to be able to bike 80 per cent of it. I don't think I've ever been so muddy – but I did bike over 80 per cent.

RANNOCH STATION TO
END OF LAND ROVER TRACK
(2 miles)

There's a hotel at Rannoch Station and a tea room in the station building. It was drizzling so we elected for a cup of tea, hoping the rain would stop.

No such luck, but the lady in the tea room told us that the man at Black Corries Lodge would like to stop people crossing the moor, but to pay no attention because it was a right of way.

As it says above, it's a Land Rover track for the first two miles. At the end of this go downhill, following a small stream. You'll then see an electricity line leading through a break in the trees.

END OF LAND ROVER TRACK
TO BLACK CORRIES LODGE
(8 miles)

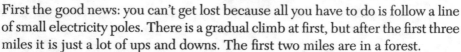

First the good news: you can't get lost because all you have to do is follow a line of small electricity poles. There is a gradual climb at first, but after the first three miles it is just a lot of ups and downs. The first two miles are in a forest.

The bad news is that there just isn't any path for the first five miles. For a determined mountain-biker this isn't necessarily a problem – it just makes it more interesting.

Basically, if you are determined and skilled you'll be able to bike most of the difficult section, providing it's dry. If it's wet you'll still be able to bike much of it, but you'll get very muddy.

There are a few interesting little traps in the form of small burns or streams that you can hardly see, but then my glasses running with water didn't help much. It wouldn't be a good idea to do the route on your own.

Don't get the idea that it was horrible, though; I hadn't enjoyed myself so much for ages! Still, if squelching axle-deep through soggy grass isn't your kind of fun, you can always walk the hard bit (it would only take a couple of hours).

Three miles short of Black Corries Lodge you hit a proper track again and things become much easier. This would be bikeable by anyone with a reasonable degree of skill.

BLACK CORRIES LODGE TO
THE KINGSHOUSE HOTEL
(3 miles)

This is quite a smooth dirt road and should be no problem at all. The first mile is fairly flat, then there is a descent for about a mile, then it flattens out somewhat.

By the time you get to the first junction, where you turn left, you'll be able to see the Kingshouse Hotel. This is the only building around, but it's generally

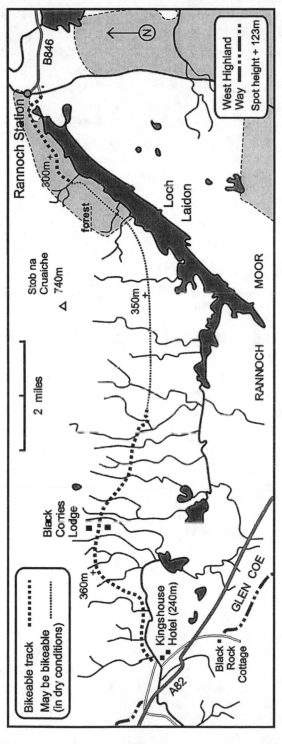

surrounded by small tents, these mostly being owned by climbers who are intent on scaling the various rock walls in Glen Coe.

As you'd expect, meals at the Kingshouse are substantial, and prices are not extravagant. The only other accommodation is further down the glen, where there is a youth hostel and a couple of regular camp sites.

CRAIGVINEAN FOREST

Two bike routes mainly on forest roads. A steep climb to start with; both routes are mostly in trees.

GENERAL INFORMATION

Craigvinean Forest is just west of Dunkeld. Access is from the A9, signposted 'The Hermitage'. There are two mountain-bike trails, a red route of nine miles and a blue route of 11 miles. Both are maintained by the Forestry Commission and are signposted.

There are some steep hills, but also quite a lot of flatter sections. There is a tourist information office (01350-727688) and a helpful mountain-bike-hire shop in Dunkeld.

Both routes are signposted at all the junctions, but some of the markers may be obscured by bracken – check the junctions carefully.

RED ROUTE
(9 miles)

Both routes start from the first car park right next to the A9. Anyone with children and a car could drive the first section to a small car park higher up in order to avoid some of the climb.

Climb through mixed forest to an S-shaped bend. Go up the hill to a Y-shaped junction and turn left, climbing steeply for about a mile. Climb up 300 metres of steep rough path, ending at a forest road junction.

Turn right here. There is a further rough path leading up from the junction – don't join this.

There are some gentler ups and downs, then, after a little over a mile, turn left on to a grassy track. This climbs steadily, then descends to another junction, where you turn left down a rough path, eventually ending back at the car park.

BLUE ROUTE
(11 miles)

This is the same as the red route until the end of the 300 metres of steep, rough path. As with the red route, turn right on to the forest road, but stay on this for two miles, ignoring the grassy track turn-off.

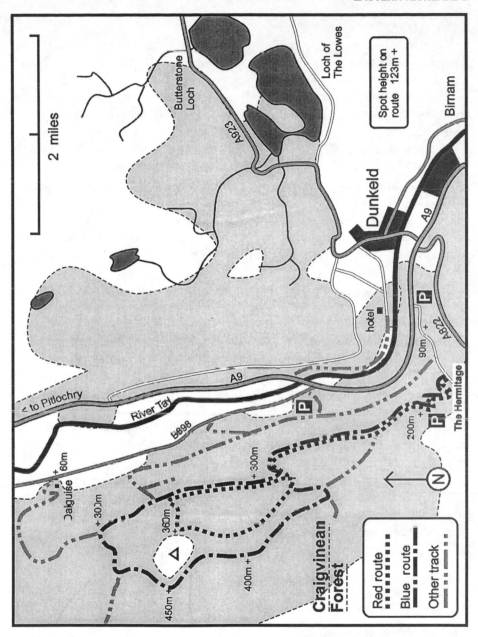

After two miles, turn left on to a forest road. This climbs steeply, with good views towards Pitlochry. After this there is a slow descent to join the red route again.

Other Options

As indicated on the map, it's possible to bike into Dunkeld using off-road trails. You have to cross the River Tay on the A9 bridge, but this is the only busy road section. The bridge over the A9 has a footpath.

Dunkeld has a wide choice of pubs and tea rooms, and there are some attractive picnic sites by the river. There is a good baker's shop in the main street which sells sandwiches and tea and coffee to take away.

To reach Dunkeld off-road you have to get yourself to the small car park on the B898. This is immediately north of the B898/A9 junction.

To reach this from the forest, turn right (east) just north of where the red and blue signposted routes diverge and follow the forest road down (see map).

Look left at the B898/A9 junction. The A9 has crossed the River Tay. Taking care, cross the main road, then cross the bridge using the footpath. Leave the road and walk down the right-hand embankment to continue downstream on a forest trail.

Continue south, keeping the river on your right. After a mile you pass a hotel. Keep by the river until the dirt surface becomes a concrete mesh, then bear left on to the access road.

Take the first left at some white painted stones. Turn right on to a minor road by a disused gatehouse. This joins the A923. Turn right on to this to enter Dunkeld.

To do this route in the opposite direction you turn left at a disused gatehouse just after the A923/minor road junction.

Alternatively you can reach the aforementioned hotel by biking through the stone arch towards the north end of Dunkeld main street. Local opinion seems to be that this is a right of way.

There is a signposted road-cycling bike route leading north from Dunkeld to Pitlochry and south from Dunkeld to Perth via Bankfoot. This is being worked on and will eventually run all the way from Perth to Inverness, with some off-road sections.

Beinn a' Ghlo Circuit

A remote 19-mile bike tour in the Grampian Mountains.

Introduction

The main route here (shorter dashes) is a circuit via Gleann Fearnach, passing to the south of Beinn a' Ghlo; virtually all of this is bikeable. The route can be made into a circle using public roads via Pitlochry. There are other possibilities, however, in Glen Tilt.

If you are prepared to walk for around three miles you could do a northern circuit linking Fealar Lodge to the top of Glen Tilt. This would create a northern loop entirely off-road. Do not bike in this area during the stalking season (Aug–Oct) without first checking locally.

A924 TO GLEN LOCH
(7 miles)

Access to the start is from the A924 nine miles east of Pitlochry. The entry point is 500 metres east of a school and a converted church. A sign says Glenfernate and Fealar Lodges and indicates that unauthorised motor vehicles are not allowed.

The road is tarmac as far as Daldhu. Bear right at the gable end of a bungalow shortly after the start to go round farm buildings, then continue up the glen. There is a gate to open and shut at the foot of a hill; after this the road rises gently all the way to Daldhu Lodge. Bear left on to a grassy Land Rover track by the river just before the lodge.

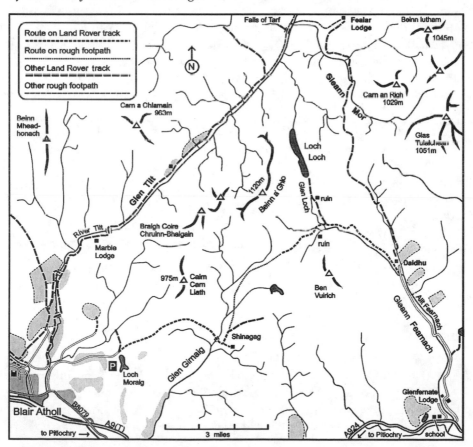

The grassy track soon gives way to a stony one. There are some ups and downs but the general trend is a gradual climb towards Beinn a' Ghlo, the track always visible in the far distance. Shortly before you cross a burn, a right fork leads up Glen Loch to the oddly named Loch Loch. This is a scenic diversion and quite short.

GLEN LOCH TO BLAIR ATHOLL
(12 miles)

After Glen Loch you pass a ruin and a steeper climb begins. The Land Rover track runs out after a couple of miles and you are on a rough footpath. Nevertheless, we found this reasonably bikeable.

You need to take care to follow the main track, which turns south after a mile or so; do not be misled into following deer tracks which lead off to the south-west and take you nowhere.

About a mile after crossing a burn, you pass through a gate and are on a faint Land Rover track leading towards Shinagag. Bear right at Shinagag, following the Land Rover track round to the north-west, crossing the Allt Girnaig burn on a small bridge.

After this there is a gentle climb, then a long descent all the way to Blair Atholl. You splash over a ford, pass a wooden hut, then go through a gate to join a tarmac surface by Loch Moraig. There is a small car park there, mostly used by fishermen.

Bear right at a tree-lined section, then descend steeply to the River Tilt. After this there is a gentler descent on the east bank of the river to the public road.

If you are doing the route in the opposite direction, note that the sign here says 'Monzie, Old Blair and Glenfender'.

GLEN TILT AND GLEANN MOR
(distances in text)

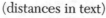

As mentioned earlier, if you are prepared to walk a bit you can create more possibilities by going by way of Fealar Lodge. Walking with a bike may seem tedious, but doing this for a mile or so often opens up distant areas to bikes. The hiking alternative would mean a camping expedition.

It's a surprise to see a remote sheep farm at Fealar Lodge; don't frighten the sheep, particularly at the spring lambing.

The section west from Fealar Lodge is only partly bikeable; you will have a better chance of doing it in a westward direction, as this is a descent.

Once you enter Glen Tilt and start to travel south from Bedford Bridge and the Falls of Tarf, some parts need care due to the steep slope.

Group from Craigmount High School at Loch Dee, Dumfries and Galloway
(page 42)

Fast descents and great views on the Ridge Route from Traquair to Yair Hill
(page 47)

Members of the party from Gracemount High School at Glen Tress
(page 44)

There are great views of the Island of Jura on the Ardnoe Route
(page 177)

The route to the Faery Isles passes several inlets on Loch Sween
(page 177)

Looking over Breadalbane from Acharn Forest near Killin
(page 85)

The Sustrans bike path by the side of Loch Venachar connects Callander routes to the Trossachs (page 80)

Bulldozed tracks put in for shooting parties mean you can bike for miles above Glen Isla (page 140)

Loch Etive on the route from Glen Kinglass
(page 156)

Passing Highland cattle in Auch Gleann
(page 160)

Scots pine regenerate naturally near Loch Gamhna in Rothiemurchus
(page 109)

Passing Buachaille Etive Mhor (Glen Coe) to cross the Black Mount
(page 153)

On the route from Fort William to Glen Coe
(page 150)

We never met a soul on the route to Loch Vaich
(page 200)

A long descent through Gleann Mor towards Amat Forest
(page 201)

Climbing through Strath Mulzie towards the scenic mountain of Seana Bhraigh
(page 203)

After just under two miles you meet the Land Rover track further south, then progress is much easier and very rapid.

The track stays on the north-west side of the river for five miles to Marble Lodge, then crosses over. A couple of miles after this it enters woodland near Gilbert's Bridge.

Staying on the east bank here is the prettier option, as this runs down by the river through mixed woodland. A mile after this you'll have to cross over anyway. Another mile or so after this you join the road at Old Bridge of Tilt, and a few minutes later you'll be in Blair Atholl.

Distances: Blair Atholl to Falls of Tarf 13 miles; Fealar Lodge to Falls of Tarf 2 miles; Falls of Tarf to Land Rover track 1.6 miles.

BLAIR ATHOLL TO GLEN BRUAR

Two circular routes, one leading to the high Minigaig pass.

INTRODUCTION

This route begins and ends at Blair Castle, seat of the Duke of Atholl. This is possibly the second most famous castle in Scotland – its attractions are too many to list here.

The route begins in woodland, then climbs steadily through open hillside towards the summit of Beinn Dearg; it then descends to a bothy.

After this you have the choice of a very steep climb towards Beinn Dearg, to return on a high-level route, or a drop to Bruar Lodge.

The Glen Bruar circle is completed by returning down Glen Bruar and Glen Banvie. This means fording a river, but you may be able to cross dry-shod if the water is low.

All of the route apart from the section between the bothy and Bruar Lodge is on Land Rover track; most of this is quite easy. The footpath may be bikeable if you are determined.

Anyone intending to do this route in September or October should first phone Atholl Estate office (01796-481355) to check for deer-stalking activities.

BLAIR CASTLE TO BOTHY

Enter the grounds of Blair Castle by the main gate. A lady in a small wooden hut charges entry for motor vehicles but bikes are free. Follow the main drive round to the castle, crossing Banvie Burn on a small bridge, then turn right.

Continue gently uphill for a little way, then turn right again where the road between the redwood trees becomes a dirt track. Immediately after, before the

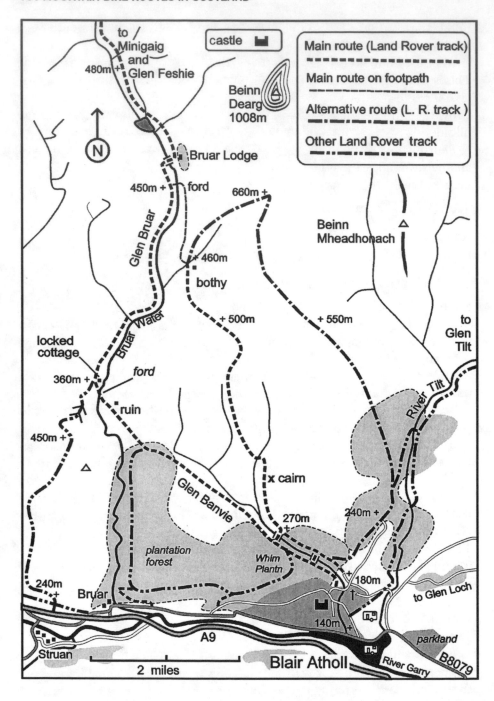

castle ▇

Main route (Land Rover track)
- - - - - - - -

Main route on footpath
—————————

Alternative route (L. R. track)
- - - - - - - -

Other Land Rover track
-·-·-·-·-

to
Minigaig
and
Glen Feshie
480m +

Beinn
Dearg
1008m

N

Bruar Lodge

450m +   ford

660m +

Beinn
Mheadhonach

+ 460m

bothy

Glen Bruar

+ 500m

+ 550m

to
Glen
Tilt

Bruar Water

locked
cottage

River Tilt

360m +   ford

· ruin

450m +

x cairn

Glen Banvie

270m +

240m +

plantation
forest

Whim
Plantn

240m +   Bruar

180m

to Glen Loch

140m +

parkland

Struan

2 miles

A9

Blair Atholl

River Garry

B8079

bridge, turn left up a hill on to a dirt track. This climbs steadily through trees, the Banvie Burn tumbling by on the right.

After two-thirds of a mile you pass an old stone bridge on the right-hand side. This is worth looking at, but continue up on the same side to the next bridge.

You pass a sign for The Whim Plantation, then reach the edge of the forest. Cross the burn here using another stone bridge and continue up on to open hillside.

Shortly after this you pass an ornamental cairn. The climb continues for another two miles after this, gradually levelling out towards its summit at 500 metres. Finally there is a drop to the bothy at the Allt Sheicheachan Burn.

RETURN BY
HIGH-LEVEL ROUTE

Until recently this route was only a footpath, but the estate has converted it into a Land Rover track. While the surface is now easier to bike, the first part is still a fierce climb.

From the bothy, follow the track which goes uphill beside the burn. The climb is gentle at first but becomes progressively steeper. At the top you are only a mile and a half from the top of Beinn Dearg and would only have another 300 metres or so of ascent to reach the summit. You'd have to leave your bike behind, though, and a compass would be advisable – the weather can change rapidly.

Travelling south now, there is a rapid descent. This levels off near the minor summit of Carn Dearg Mor, then there is a long, fast descent over three miles.

At the end of this you are in forest at Blairuachdar Wood. Turn left here to a tarmac road and descend to a crossroads. Go straight over to return to the start.

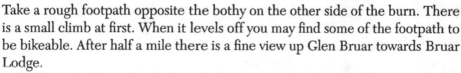

BOTHY TO GLEN BRUAR,
GLEN BANVIE AND RETURN

Take a rough footpath opposite the bothy on the other side of the burn. There is a small climb at first. When it levels off you may find some of the footpath to be bikeable. After half a mile there is a fine view up Glen Bruar towards Bruar Lodge.

Half a mile from the Lodge there is a sign directing walkers round the grounds. Obey this and turn left towards the river.

Providing the water level is reasonably low you are best to ford the river at this point, as this will get you on to the Land Rover track on the other side. If the water level is high, continue walking your bike for a further half-mile to the bridge by the lodge.

It is possible to ride your bike for a further three miles upstream; beyond this exploration must be on foot. Mountain-bikers do occasionally go further than this, pushing or carrying their bikes up the hill to the Minigaig, then biking/ walking on to Glen Feshie and Speyside. This, however, is a major expedition, and warm, waterproof clothing, OS map and compass are essential.

Return south by following the track down Glen Bruar to the locked cottage at Cuilltemhuc. A grassy track leads over from there to a ford and to Glen Banvie; 100 metres upstream there are some natural stepping stones where you may be able to get over with dry feet. If the river is high do not cross, but return via Bruar (see map).

The last section is a short climb to Glen Banvie; turn left in pine woods, then drop to the start. The surface is quite loose to begin with, and you need to watch your speed in the trees as there might be a vehicle round the corner.

THE GAICK PASS

A high-level route between Perthshire and the Spey Valley (21 miles).

GENERAL NOTES

Looking at a map of Scotland, one might wonder why General Wade did not use the Gaick, rather than the Pass of Drumochter, when planning his route north. The Gaick has much the same elevation and is more direct, although the reason was possibly the threat of winter avalanches on the steeper slopes of the Gaick.

Subsequent road and rail engineers continued with the Wade line, so the current A9 and the railway line sweep to the west, leaving the lonely Gaick to the occasional walker and mountain-biker.

The route is a right of way, although it may be impassable in winter because of snow. Even in summer take warm, waterproof clothing. It's best to bike it with a friend.

It's probably most convenient to do the route in a northern direction, as you finish near Kingussie, which has a good bus service (roughly every hour) back to the start (although buses don't take bikes). Trains are less frequent. At the time of writing there was some possibility of a special bike-bus service being started to carry cyclists between the Kingussie area and Pitlochry. Phone Pitlochry Tourist Information to enquire (01796-472215).

NORTHBOUND
(21 miles)

Start from the A9 at the Trinafour turn-off, ten miles north of Blair Atholl near Dalnacardoch Lodge. Directly opposite the junction a locked gate leads to a dirt road leading up the hill, signposted Public Footpath by Gaick to Speyside.

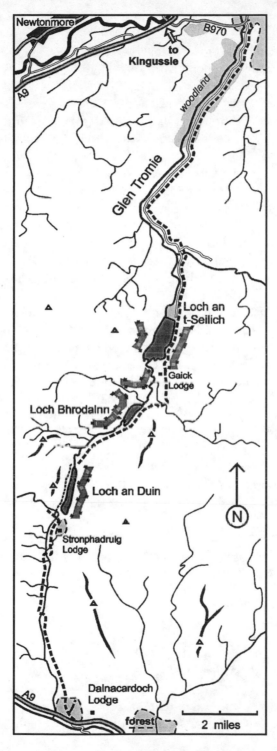

If you have a car, leave it at the lay-by 500 metres further south on the same side of the road.

The dirt road climbs through trees above the A9 snow gate. There is a right turning which you should ignore. After this the dirt road leaves the wood by a radio mast. It then becomes a rough track.

Ignore a left turn which drops down to the burn, then pass through a gate by a ruined cottage, a tall cairn on the left. After this the track drops to the burn, passing another (intact) cottage, then crosses the burn to the west side on a wooden bridge.

The track climbs steadily; splash across the burn again on a concrete ford, then pass Stronphadruig Lodge (unoccupied) standing in trees on the right. The long dam-like feature ahead is a glacial moraine and the first loch lies on the other side.

The track curves round to the left, then crosses the burn. Splash across this ford, then, 200 metres after, leave the track, carrying your bike over a small burn and then going up the side of the glacial moraine. There is a tiny cairn by the track at this point.

Once you have gained sight of Loch an Duin the path along the west side will be visible. This can be biked in parts but care is necessary, owing to the steep sides. Towards the north end of the loch the path becomes easier.

At the end of the loch, if it's safe, cross the river that flows out of it. If the water is low you might make it across dry-shod, otherwise it's a wading job. Boulders and gravel make cycling across impossible.

Once you are on the other side of the river you'll meet a Land Rover track; from here it's a fast descent to Loch Bhrodainn. Here Gaick Lodge comes into view, together with a little bridge over the river.

Ignore this and keep on the Land Rover track, climbing up by trees and a deer fence, then descending again to the Allt Garbh burn. Assuming the water level is reasonable, it's possible to bike across this. Turn left downstream after crossing the burn.

The track continues past the lodge; it would probably be tactful not to have your picnic lunch opposite. Keep on past Loch an t-Seilich, cycling up and down through trees to reach the estate road at the far end, by the dam.

After this it's eight miles on the estate road to Tromie Bridge, then another three miles on the B970 to Kingussie. A locked gate on the estate road prevents cars coming up; you can bike round it.

SOUTHBOUND
(21 miles)

To do the route in a southerly direction, start at the bridge over the River Tromie, two miles east of Kingussie. A dirt road leads through trees next to the bridge. Cunningly, the estate has left the first 400 metres unsurfaced in an effort to convince you it doesn't go anywhere much.

The white hatched area next to the bridge is to allow Forestry Commission timber lorries to turn. If you have a car, park it on the other side of the bridge.

The road follows the east bank of the River Tromie, initially through woods; it then emerges on to open hillside. Shortly after this you pass Bhran Cottage on your right by the river. A mile after this bear right, to cross the river on a small bridge.

A mile after Gaick Lodge bear right, crossing the burn to keep on the Land Rover track. After passing the second loch there is a steady climb to Loch an Duin. The Land Rover track runs out 200 metres before the loch. If it's safe, ford the river where it leaves the loch to gain access to the track on the west side.

PASS OF RYVOAN

A long, circular mountain-bike route with great views and some challenging sections.

The Pass of Ryvoan runs between Glen More, near Aviemore, and Nethybridge. It climbs to 380 metres, mostly through natural Caledonian pine woods. There are good views of the Cairngorm Mountains and Glenmore Forest Park. Experienced mountain-bikers will be able to cycle the whole thing; anyone inexperienced or with another type of bike will have to walk in places. Description is circular, starting from Aviemore.

It is usually possible to do this route all the year round provided it is not snow-covered. Waterproof clothing is advisable at any time, but in winter you should be prepared for bad weather with extra warm clothing, woolly hat, gloves, etc. Total distance right round is 25 miles; Nethybridge to Glenmore via Ryvoan is 10 miles.

**PASS OF RYVOAN
CIRCULAR**
(25 miles from
Coylumbridge)

Starting in Aviemore, take the ski road towards Cairngorm. After a mile you pass Inverdruie, which has a mountain-bike hire shop and the Gallery Tea Room.

At Coylumbridge, a mile further on, you have the option of turning left, to do the outward journey to Nethybridge on the B970, or continuing on towards Loch Morlich and using trails via An Slugan.

The B970 is fairly quiet with good views. Whether you take the public road

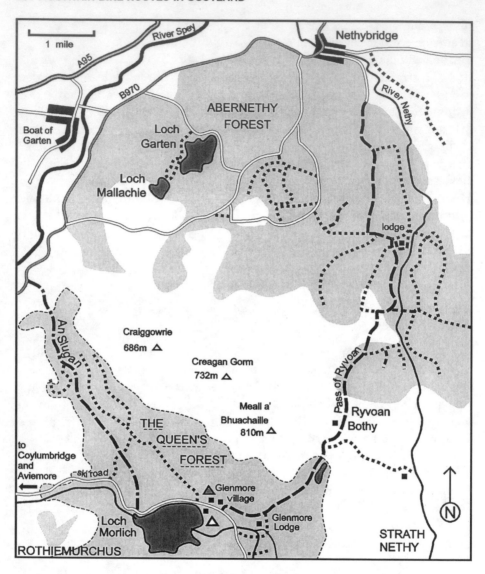

or the An Slugan route, you should also go via Abernethy Forest and Loch Garten.

Abernethy Forest, like Rothiemurchus further south, is a remnant of the native Scots pine forest that once covered the Highlands, habitat of red squirrel, wildcat, pine marten and red deer. Ospreys were re-established near Loch Garten in the 1950s; a helping factor was the free lunch available to them from Rothiemurchus fish farm.

Nethybridge has a tea room and craft shop on the left as you enter the village. Bar lunches are available at the hotel.

In Nethybridge, take the minor road between the post office and the River Nethy, travelling west. This climbs gently, then turns south to the forest, becoming a track.

Keep straight on, ignoring any left turns, until you come to a T-junction, where you can go no further. Turn left here to travel east, then take the second turning to the right (south). If you meet the forest lodge, which is private, you have missed the turning.

There is a fork in the track near here; you can take either way. The right-hand trail (different pattern on the map) takes a rather higher line on the approach to the pass. It drops down again on a track that may be muddy. Both paths climb steadily, sometimes steeply, and are now winding and more difficult, rather than just being forest trails.

When you leave the trees, most of the climbing is done. Cairngorm will be visible ahead, and you may see skiers on it if it's winter and your eyesight is good enough.

The path becomes rocky and more Scots pine appears, then, after reaching open country again, you pass Ryvoan Bothy. Usually there will be someone camping there.

Shortly after this there is a difficult steep descent, more like a river bed than a path, and after this a left turn leading towards Bynack Stable. This is not a stable, but another bothy.

The path to Bynack Stable is mostly bikeable, but cycling any further than this, for example up Strath Nethy, is completely impossible.

Continuing south, the path enters Glenmore Forest Park. Despite being sandy in places it is quite fast (be considerate to walkers) and mainly downhill.

Soon you pass Lochan Uaine, with steep crags above, then drop to a small bridge. After this, at Glenmore Lodge, the track finally becomes a road.

Turn right at the ski road to return to Aviemore. Reward yourself with an applestrudel at the Glenmore shop tea room; this is beside Glenmore Camp Site.

There are more bike trails to the south of Loch Morlich and in Rothiemurchus. It would be possible to make this route even longer by including these.

ABERNETHY FOREST

The tracks around Abernethy Forest are not too hilly and have quite reasonable surfaces, so would be very suitable for families. Biking round the forest could be combined with a visit to the RSPB hide near Loch Garten to see the ospreys, or a picnic by Loch Garten or Loch Mallachie. Refer to the map.

AROUND ROTHIEMURCHUS

Varied mountain-biking in native pine forests.

Rushing rivers, native pine forests, a variety of mountain-biking – you can see why this area is popular.

For the adventurous, the trip to Loch Einich will provide a technical challenge, and a view of the remote loch will be long remembered. For families, the trails around Loch an Eilein and south of Loch Morlich will provide good days in beautiful scenery, the dramatic backdrop of the Cairngorms never far away.

LOCH AN EILEIN TO LOCH MORLICH
(5 miles)

The description assumes that you start from Loch an Eilein, but access is also possible from Inverdruie or Loch Morlich. There is a visitor centre at Loch an Eilein giving information about the Cairngorms (there are also toilets and a car park). Loch an Eilein means 'loch of the island' in Gaelic. The castle on the island dates from the twelfth century.

Leave the visitor centre, cross the river, then bear right following the loch shore. After a mile take a left turn to leave the loch. The other path goes right round; however, Rothiemurchus Estate asks that you do not bike round. It is possible to gain access to Glen Feshie via forest paths to the south of Loch an Eilein. If you want to do this, walk the short section after the turn-off (see next route).

The first problem is a locked gate. People hiring mountain-bikes at Inverdruie Mountain Bikes get the key. Those using their own bikes can get a key for a £5 deposit. It is possible to get your bike over the gate, but if this is too difficult, wait a little; someone with a key may be along shortly. After the gate, continue east along a sandy trail to the first junction: Lochan Deo. Turn right here (south) to go to Glen Einich, or keep straight on for Loch Morlich.

The journey to Loch Morlich is not entirely smooth; the track gets rough in places. You have to carry your bike over the Cairngorm Club Footbridge. Shortly after the bridge there is another junction in the path, incongruously named Piccadilly.

The right turn here leads up to the Lairig Ghru, the most famous mountain pass in Scotland. This pass takes you from Speyside to Braemar, a distance of over 20 miles. It rises to 835 metres. Walter Poucher, writing in 1947, said that a bicycle was a disadvantage and this is still true, despite improvements in bike technology.

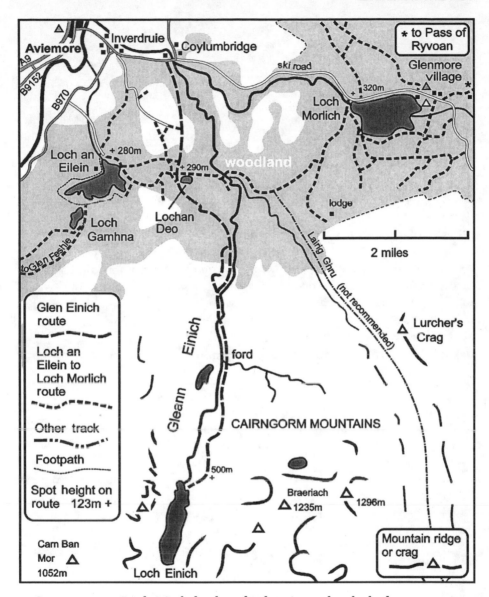

Continuing to Loch Morlich, though, there's another locked gate – a more serious one this time, with a deer fence. If you haven't got the key, getting over the stile is possible, but it helps if there is more than one of you. There's a wee gate for dogs.

Turn left at a forest road leading to Rothiemurchus Lodge. A mile after this you reach Loch Morlich. Turn right just before the public road to gain access to the Loch Morlich trails (see map). There is a shop and tea room by the camp site at Glenmore village.

Lochan Deo
to Glen Einich
(12 miles return distance)

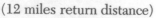

Unlike the Lairig Ghru, the path up Glen Einich is bikeable. The trip to Loch Einich is quite long and requires you to wade across a river carrying your bike. Keep to the path in the deer-stalking season (Sept–Oct).

Get to Lochan Deo as described in the previous section and turn south. The track at first is a steady climb through natural Scots pine forest; eventually this thins out, giving good views up the glen.

Near the edge of the forest the path divides into two. The estate has had to create a higher route, as the lower track slid into the river. The lower track is quicker, providing you can negotiate the landslides.

Further up there is a narrow single-plank footbridge, which needs care. Further on still, you need to wade across a river. Due to a combination of depth, width and boulders in the river bed, biking across is impossible. Your reward for this is the view over the remote loch with its high cliffs plunging from the summit of Sgoran Dubh Mhor to the surface of the loch 600 metres below.

Distances: Loch An Eilein to Loch Einich and return 15 miles; Loch An Eilein to Loch Morlich 5 miles; Inverdruie to Coylumbridge via Loch an Eilein 5 miles.

Some Useful Phone Numbers
Loch Morlich Youth Hostel: 01479-861238
Aviemore Youth Hostel: 01479-810345
Inverdruie Mountain-Bikes: 01479-810787
Aviemore Tourist Information: 01479-810363
Glenmore Camp Site: 01479-861271

Loch an Eilean to Glen Feshie

It's a pity more aren't like this – a bike route passing through ancient Caledonian pine woods.

Introduction
The Scots pine woods here aren't just a historic remnant of how Scotland used to be – they're also extremely beautiful. Too often we only appreciate what we once had when we have lost it. Scotland is still beautiful, of course, but when she was clothed in her ancient forests she must have been just wonderful. Perhaps one day we will have them back.

This route is fairly short and it isn't hilly. It forms a useful link between routes around Loch Morlich and the route leading to Braemar.

Quite apart from the scenery, it's a fun route to do because the track meanders interestingly through the trees. The bit round Loch an Eilean is a nature walk recommended for children. Walk if there's anyone about.

Loch an Eilean
to Feshiebridge
(6 miles)

Access to Loch an Eilean is from the B970 running from Inverdruie to Feshie-bridge or from trails around Loch Morlich further east (see previous route).

There is a visitor centre at Loch an Eilean, giving general information about the Cairngorms. There are also toilets and a car park.

Leave the visitor centre, cross the river where it flows out of the loch, then bear right, following the loch shore. After about a mile you come to a fork in the track. The left turn takes you towards Loch Morlich; bear right to continue round the loch.

The path on this next section is less wide and forms a nature trail used by young children. If there is anyone about, dismount and walk. I did this last time and a lady passing by said: 'And they're supposed to be able to ride their bikes on mountains!' If this happens to you, just smile.

You have to leave the trail round Loch an Eilean and cut south to Loch Gamhna. This isn't signposted; it's a left turn 100 metres after crossing a wee burn.

Once you get to Loch Gamhna you have to make another left turn, otherwise you'll end up going right round Loch Gamhna and back to Loch an Eilean. Turn left at the first junction.

This next section is a narrow winding path with lots of new Scots pine trees. These are springing up naturally because the area is protected by deer fencing. There are too many deer in Scotland and they kill all the young trees in winter by eating the new shoots. Wolves – that's what we need!

Anyway, you pass a small bothy, then see the spruce trees of a plantation forest just ahead. Enter the forest.

The path becomes a forest road; bear left at a blue cross-country skiing marker post and continue straight on for a mile, taking the second left at a four-ways junction for Feshiebridge. You get to the public road opposite some wooden chalets or huts. Turn left here to go up Glen Feshie.

Feshiebridge to
Upper Glen Feshie
(8 miles, to Landseer's Bothy)

While there are forest roads in the woods in Glen Feshie, none of them will take you up the glen. Use the minor road that leads past Glen Feshie Hostel to Achlean.

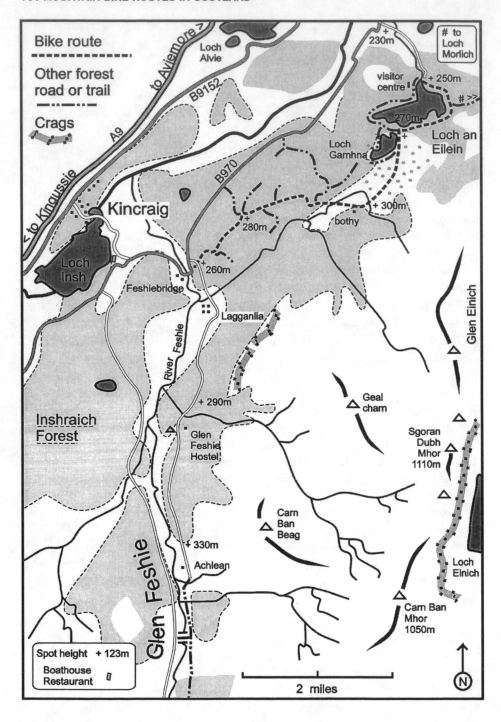

Bike route

Other forest
road or trail

Crags

to Aviemore 7

Loch
Alvie

B9152

A9

to
Loch
Morlich

+ 230m

visitor
centre

+ 250m

>>

270m

Loch an
Eilein

Loch
Gamhna

+

B970

< to Kingussie

Kincraig

Loch
Insh

+ 280m

bothy

+ 300m

+ 260m

Feshiebridge

Lagganlia

River Feshie

Inshraich
Forest

+ 290m

Glen
Feshie
Hostel

+ 330m

Achlean

Glen Feshie

Glen Einich

Geal
charn

Sgoran
Dubh
Mhor
1110m

Carn
Ban
Beag

Loch
Einich

Carn Ban
Mhor
1050m

Spot height + 123m

Boathouse
Restaurant

2 miles

N

The road ends at Achlean; two tracks lead off from here. One goes up the hill to the mountain Carn Ban Mor; this is not bikeable. The other goes up the glen, and you can bike this.

Continuing in the same direction as the road, the path leads between a small hill and a cottage. After this it crosses a burn, then leads over a flat area with grass and heather. You pass a ruined cottage, then come to a bridge over the river.

You can either cross the bridge and continue up on the surfaced road, or you can continue on the same side of the river using forest tracks.

To do the latter, continue in the same direction, cross another burn, then enter plantation forest on a path about 200 metres away from the River Feshie.

After a mile or so the plantation forest gives way to natural woodland. To continue after this, just keep following the most obvious path on the east bank of the river. Eventually there is another bridge, and if you continue up after this you reach Landseer's Bothy. You've probably seen his *Monarch of the Glen* somewhere . . .

You can continue for miles after this, all the way to Braemar (see next route).

LOCAL FACILITIES

The only eating place in the vicinity is The Boathouse Restaurant at Loch Insh, just east of Kincraig. There is a shop in Kincraig.

BRAEMAR TO GLEN FESHIE

A remote bike route connecting Deeside to the Spey Valley.

INTRODUCTION

While this route is not particularly hilly, it does cover some remote country. Taking OS Landranger map sheet 43 and a compass is advisable.

Warm, waterproof clothing and some emergency food is necessary at any time of year. The route will be very exposed in bad weather and the only two buildings offering effective shelter are the Geldie Bothy and Landseer's Bothy (see map). There is no real shelter in the middle section. Total distance (Linn of Dee to Achlean) is 22 miles.

The greater part of the route is on Land Rover track; the section between Geldie Lodge and Linn of Dee is comparatively easy. There is a six-mile section in the middle which is a rough footpath; parts of this will have to be walked.

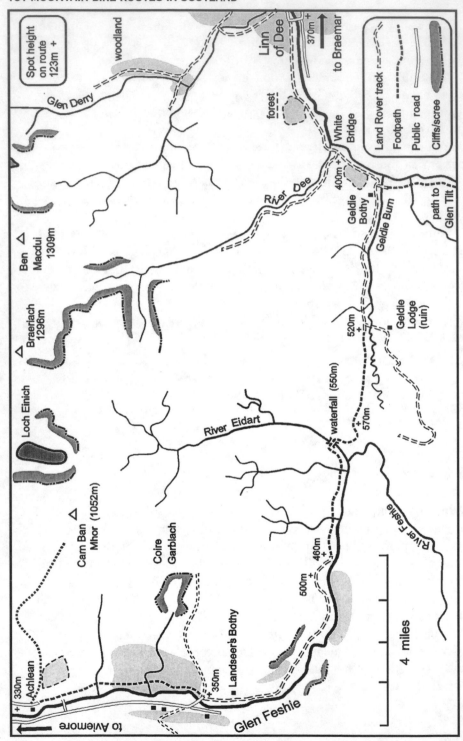

LINN OF DEE TO GELDIE BURN

(5 miles)

Start at Linn of Dee, which is six miles west of Braemar. From the north side of the bridge take the track which leads west, signposted 'Public Footpath Glen Geldie and Glen Tilt'.

The path runs along the north bank of the River Dee through some Scots pine. After this there are fine open views. You pass a plantation forest, then come to White Bridge.

Turning right will take you up the Lairig Ghru; people do take bikes up there, but having a bike in the Lairig Ghru is a disadvantage. Cross the bridge and bear left to travel south on the Land Rover track.

You pass another small plantation forest, then meet a fork in the river. Turn right (west) here, and follow the north bank of the Geldie Burn by a corrugated-iron-roofed cottage with no windows (Geldie Bothy).

GELDIE BURN TO RIVER EIDART

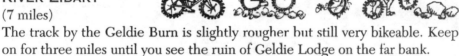

(7 miles)

The track by the Geldie Burn is slightly rougher but still very bikeable. Keep on for three miles until you see the ruin of Geldie Lodge on the far bank.

The track leads across the burn, but don't cross. Instead take a rough footpath to continue west. How bikeable it is will depend on how wet the ground is; we found we could bike about 80 per cent of it.

After two miles you see Glen Feshie ahead, but the path becomes less distinct. There is a tiny sign saying Glen Feshie, and a few small cairns.

If you miss these, just keep on, staying at the same height, until you meet the River Eidart. There is a bridge erected by the Scottish Rights of Way Society. This is by a waterfall, which you normally hear before you see. Search for it if necessary; don't try to ford the river.

RIVER EIDART TO GLEN FESHIE

(10 miles to Achlean)

After the bridge the path is easy to follow and, after a little way, more bikeable. There is a final difficult section and then you are on Land Rover track again.

The track follows the east bank of the River Feshie for four miles. Initially there is a steep climb, then there is a steep descent. After this the path is fairly gentle, passing through attractive scenery with lots of Scots pine.

The river runs through a ravine; a mile after this it passes Landseer's Bothy at Ruigh Aiteachain. This has recently been renovated by the Scottish Mountain Bothy Association. Staying here is free, but you will need a sleeping bag. If you are lucky there will be firewood. Do not cut local trees.

The track then crosses the river and becomes a surfaced road. A footpath continues north on the east bank; this passes through attractive woodland.

On the west side of the river, the public road starts at a gate which may be locked to prevent entry by cars.

Continuing on to Aviemore is best done by using the B970 to Inverdruie by way of Feshiebridge (off map). There is a restaurant at The Boathouse at Loch Insh, and a food shop at Kincraig.

ACCOMMODATION

Glen Feshie Hostel (01540-651323) is a good place to stay; to get there, cross the river just south of Achlean at the second bridge and follow a footpath north to the road. The hostel is two miles further north.

The Boathouse at Loch Insh also has a variety of accommodation options (01540-651272).

Braemar has lots of accommodation choices, including a number of hotels and B&Bs (tourist information: 013397-41600). There is also a youth hostel (013397-41659).

In addition there is a smaller youth hostel one mile east of Linn of Dee at Inverey (no phone).

EASTERN CAIRNGORMS

A two- or three-day circular mountain-bike route in Scotland's biggest mountains.

PLEASE NOTE

Take warm, waterproof clothing; the weather can change rapidly. If you can't complete the first section in daylight, you need to camp. Total distance is 58 miles. OS Landranger map 36 and a compass are essential.

TOMINTOUL TO BRAEMAR
(35 miles)

This is remote country, and there is a wet river crossing. You may have to wheel your bike about five miles and carry it for some of this.

Day One: Turn right off the A939 just south of Tomintoul, signposted Delnabo. Follow the minor road, turning left to a track before the road crosses the River Avon (Queen's View sign, parking). Continue upstream on the east bank of the

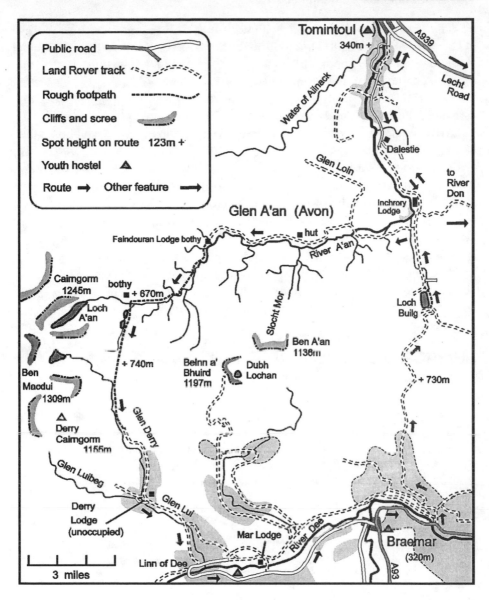

Public road

Land Rover track

Rough footpath

Cliffs and scree

Spot height on route   123m +

Youth hostel   △

Route   ➡   Other feature   ➡

Tomintoul (△)
340m +

A939

Lecht
Road

Water of Ailnack

Dalestie

Glen Loin

to
River
Don

Inchrory
Lodge

Glen A'an (Avon)

hut

Faindouran Lodge bothy

River A'an

Cairngorm
1245m

bothy
■ + 670m

Loch
A'an

Slocht Mor

Loch
Builg

Ben A'an
1138m

+ 740m

Beinn a'
Bhuird
1197m

Dubh
Lochan

+ 730m

Ben
Macdui
1309m

△
Derry
Cairngorm
1155m

Glen Derry

Glen Luibeg

Derry
Lodge
(unoccupied)

Glen Lui

Mar Lodge

River Dee

Braemar
(320m)

A93

Linn of Dee

3 miles

river. The other tarmac road crosses again and you roll along in pleasant scenery, thinking 'this is easy'. The tarmac ends at Dalestie, five miles from the start; keep on to Inchrory Lodge.

You can turn east here up a little gorge to the source of the River Don and then follow this, but don't. Instead continue south past the lodge. Turn right (west) over a small bridge crossing the Builg Burn just before it enters the River Avon.

The track passes the Linn of Avon waterfall, then crosses to the north bank at the foot of Glen Loin. Here the track climbs steeply to avoid a waterlogged lower path. On the upper path, ignore the right turn to Glen Loin.

The pleasant wooded countryside gives way to larger mountains. Continue west on the north bank of the river, past the dramatic corrie of Slochd Mor. The small hut here is a useful shelter and a good place for your first break.

After this the track climbs to avoid a river gorge then descends to cross a burn. Soon, at Faindouran Lodge bothy, the Land Rover track becomes a rough path. This may be bikeable in places. It crosses a wide valley then leads through a narrow ravine to the rough shelter at the Fords of Avon.

You need to cross the stepping stones here to continue south to Glen Derry. If you have time, leave your bike and walk one mile further west to Loch A'an (Avon). This remote loch with its huge cliffs, dropping down from Cairngorm, is one of the most dramatic in Scotland; it is an interesting place to camp.

Crossing the river when the water level is low is not too difficult; people have been killed trying to cross when the river was high. After this there is a tiny bikeable bit, a smaller burn to cross, then three miles of boulders before the path becomes bikeable again opposite Corrie Etchachan.

After a further mile the path becomes Land Rover track. Keep on the east side of the river and enter old pine woods at the south end of Glen Derry. When you encounter unoccupied Derry Lodge, bear left to go south-east down Glen Lui.

Two miles later, turn right to cross a bridge, passing through more woods to the public road. Turn right to the Linn of Dee, then left to travel east to Braemar.

At the time of writing it was possible to cycle on the north bank of the river through Mar Estate; however, the Victoria Bridge, next to Mar Lodge, is normally locked. This means you have to continue three miles past Braemar to the Invercauld Bridge to cross the river.

BRAEMAR TO TOMINTOUL
(23 miles)

Day Two: Unlike day one, virtually all of this is bikeable. The exception is the footpath on the east side of Loch Builg.

Start at Braemar, taking the A93 towards Ballater for three miles, then, 200 metres after crossing the river, turn left, signposted Keilloch. After 300 metres turn left through Aldourie Farm. This becomes a dirt road; there is an electricity line on the left. Shortly after, you enter forest and the electricity line ends. Very soon after this, turn right up a Land Rover track. If you meet a cattle grid you have missed the turning.

Route-finding thereafter is easy – just keep going. The biking is more difficult

– it is a big climb – but there are panoramic views. The track continues to ruined Lochbuilg Lodge, but leave it and take the footpath on the east side of the loch.

The track down Glen Builg is a ten-mile descent to Tomintoul.

Hostels: Braemar (013397-41659), Tomintoul (01807-580282) and Inverey (no phone).

Bike hire: Braemar Outdoor Centre (013397-41242).

Braemar Tourist Information: 013397-41600.

GLENLIVET MOUNTAIN-BIKE TRAILS

Often hilly, these circular bike routes offer fine views and a sense of open space.

These signposted bike routes are interesting to explore, but can also be used as part of a long-distance mountain-bike route, connecting the Speyside Way to other routes in the Cairngorms.

Do not bike on the Ladder or Cromdale Hills, as summit vegetation and wildlife is easily disturbed. OS map sheet 36 might be useful. Tomintoul Tourist Information: 01807-580285.

ROUTE 1
(10 miles)

Can be muddy and narrow in places. From the start at the north end of Tomintoul, take the A939 north-west and cross the Bridge of Avon. Turn left at a stop sign, pass a lodge, then Stronachavie. Before reaching Burn of Brown, turn right (north) on to a track to Bridge of Brown (where there is a tea room). Turn right to the A939.

After half a mile leave it again and turn right by a car park on to a forest track. When you meet the A939 again, go on a little, then turn left on to a minor road. Follow this north for two miles, by the west bank of the River Avon, to a footbridge (# on map).

Cross the river and follow a track downstream past a field to the B9136. Join a farm road and travel south-east, past Achlichnie Farm and Tomachlaggan, then turn left (north-east) on to a forest road.

The first two right turns are a loop round the hill; take the third right, at the edge of the forest by Chabet Water. Follow this upstream (south). At Glenconglass Farm turn right then left (south), following Conglass Water upstream towards Tomintoul. At a sharp left bend near The Old Kennels join the Speyside Way, passing under an electricity line to the start.

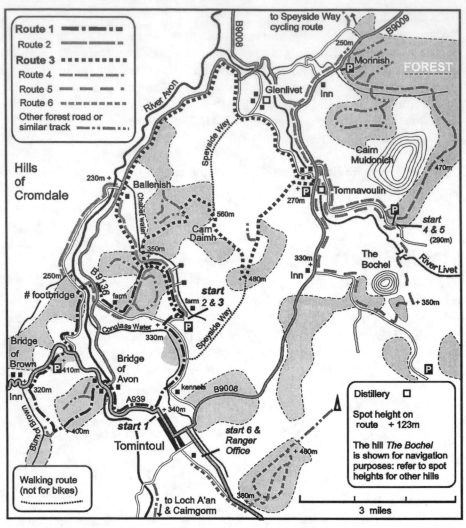

Map legend:

- **Route 1** ▬ ▬ ▬ ▬
- Route 2 ▬▬▬
- **Route 3** ■ ■ ■ ■ ■
- Route 4 ▬ ▬ ▬
- Route 5 ▬ ▬ ▬ ▪
- Route 6 ▬ ▬ ▬ ▬
- Other forest road or similar track ▬ ▪ ▬ ▪

to Speyside Way cycling route

B9008 B9009

FOREST

250m

Morinish

Glenlivet   Inn

River Avon

Speyside Way

Cairn Muldonich +470m

Hills of Cromdale

230m +

Ballenish

+ P 270m   □ Tomnavoulin

P start 4 & 5 (290m)

560m

Carn Daimh

350m +

330m + Inn

The Bochel

River Livet

+ 350m

250m +

B9136

farm

+ 480m

footbridge

Conglass Water +

start 2 & 3

farm

P

330m

Speyside Way

Bridge of Brown +

P 410m

Bridge of Avon

kennels   B9008

P

320m

Inn

Burn of Brown

A939

+ 340m

Distillery □

Spot height on route + 123m

The hill *The Bochel* is shown for navigation purposes: refer to spot heights for other hills

+ 400m

start 1

Tomintoul

start 6 & Ranger Office

+ 480m

Walking route (not for bikes)

to Loch A'an & Cairngorm

380m +

3 miles

ADDITIONAL INFORMATION

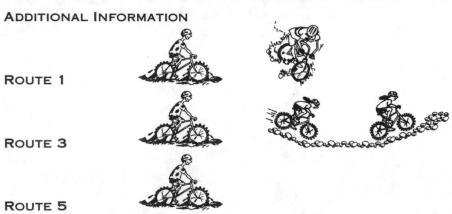

ROUTE 1

ROUTE 3

ROUTE 5

ROUTE 3

(15 miles)

Can be stony and muddy in places. Start as for route 2 but turn right (north) to cross Chabet Water in trees two-thirds of a mile after the second farm turn-off, keeping in the forest. After crossing the river, travel two miles in the forest, then bear right (south) by the Speyside Way to the summit of Carn Daimh. Join the Speyside Way.

Turn left (north) at the next junction, leaving the Speyside Way. Eventually turn left (north) on to the B9008 at Tomnavoulin. After a short distance turn left (north-west) towards Glenlivet. Bear left at Blairfindy Lodge Hotel, then left on to the B9136. Keeping on this, curve round to the south. After three miles, ignore the right turn over the River Avon but soon after turn left at Ballenish House, then continue south up a track, initially through woods, then on to open hillside. Keep straight on through the forest, following the south bank of Chabet Water to complete the route.

ROUTE 4

(11 miles)

Smooth forest roads. From the car park, head towards Tomnavoulin a little way, then turn right into the forest. The route climbs the shoulder of Cairn Muldonich, then descends to cross the Allt a' Choileachain burn, before turning north-west (red squirrel markers) towards the Morinish forest car park on the B9009.

Turn left (south-west) on to the public road, then left again on to the B9008. Just before Tomnavoulin bear left on to the minor road leading to the start point.

ROUTE 2

(7 miles)

Mostly hard surfaces. From Glenconglass car park follow a dirt road north past two farms to a forest. Ignore all left and right turns. Leave the forest on a hill track, passing a ruin, then drop to the B9136 at Ballenish. Turn right (north) on to the road, but after 200 metres turn left over the river. Travel upstream (south) for two and a half miles, then cross the river on the footbridge. Follow directions from route 1 (#) to return to your starting point

ROUTE 5

(10 miles)

Head south on a farm track from the car park for a little way, then cross the River Livet on a footbridge (if you meet a steel gate, you've missed the turning). Go south through a field with marker posts, the conical hill of The Bochel to the right.

Follow the line of the fence to an electricity line and a house, then join a farm track. Go through another gate, pass another house, then turn right through the

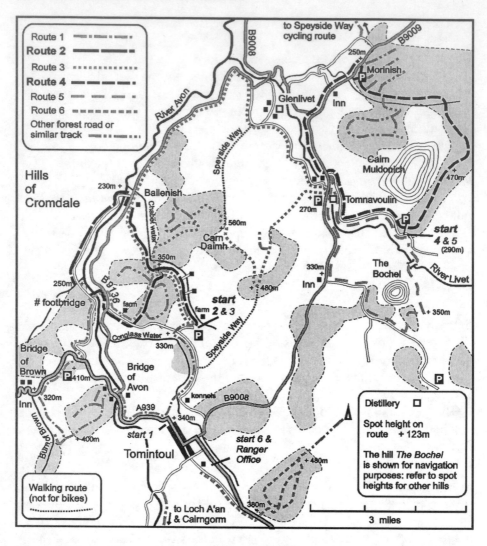

forest to the public road. Descend to the B9008. This route can be muddy in wet conditions. The Pole Inn at the junction does good food at reasonable prices.

Turn right on to the B9008 and right just after Tomnavoulin to return to the start.

ROUTE 6
(Quite short)

Mostly on smooth forest roads. This is just south of Tomintoul and explores a small area in some detail. The entry point is in Glenmulliach Forest, just south of Tomintoul.

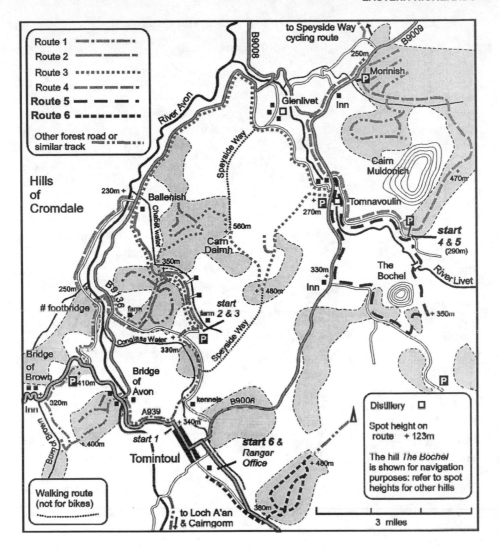

Route 1
Route 2
Route 3
Route 4
Route 5
Route 6

Other forest road or
similar track

Hills
of
Cromdale

to Speyside Way
cycling route

B9008

B9009

250m

Morinish
P

Glenlivet
Inn

Speyside Way

River Avon

Cairn
Muldonich
470m

230m +

Ballenish

Chabbt Water

560m

Carn
Daimh

350m

270m

Tomnavoulin
P

P

start
4 & 5
(290m)

River Livet

330m

The
Bochel

Inn

+ 480m

250m

B9136

footbridge

farm

farm
start
2 & 3

Speyside Way

+ 350m

Conglass Water

330m

P

Bridge
of
Brown

P 410m

Inn

320m

+ 400m

start 1

Tomintoul

Bridge
of
Avon

A939

kennels

B9008

+ 340m

start 6 &
Ranger
Office

P

Distillery ☐

Spot height on
route   + 123m

The hill *The Bochel*
is shown for navigation
purposes: refer to spot
heights for other hills

Walking route
(not for bikes)

Burn of Brown

+ 480m

to Loch A'an
& Cairngorm

380m

3 miles

THE SPEYSIDE WAY

Spey Bay to Craigellachie

A long-distance route using an old rail line, and river and forest tracks.

GENERAL NOTES ON THE SPEYSIDE WAY

The Speyside Way runs from Spey Bay to Tomintoul. Bikes are allowed on it except for a section south of Ballindalloch where the route crosses a fragile upland area. There is a good off-road alternative to this for mountain-bikes.

The route is surprisingly quiet but very varied. Some sections are on the old Strathspey Railway, other parts are in forest; the latter are very hilly. The route also uses riverside paths and the occasional minor road.

The nearest railway stations are at Elgin and Keith; there is also a special bus service called the Speyside Rambler which calls at various points on the way. At the time of writing it didn't take bikes, but it might be very useful for returning you to your car at the end of a trip.

The local ranger service issues an annual newsletter called The Speyside Wayfarer. This gives information updates on the state of the Way, and is full of advertisements for B&Bs, hotels, places to eat and places to buy food. The phone number of the ranger service is 01340-881266.

SPEY BAY TO FOCHABERS
(5 miles)

The Speyside Way starts near the Tugnet Ice House (now a museum) at Spey Bay. You can get to this on the B9104 from Fochabers. Join a stony track by Tugnet House, just east of the ice house.

A more interesting way to get to the start is from Garmouth by using a former railway line and an old viaduct. Take the B9105 from Mosstodloch to Garmouth and join the Spey Viaduct Walk by picnic tables as you enter the village. The former rail line joins the main route just south of the start.

After this keep straight on unless the thistle waymark symbols indicate otherwise. It's easy to miss these on a bike if you are travelling quickly.

There is a left fork in trees after a mile, then you meet the river. After passing some fishing huts, look for a little ramp leaving the main trail by a horse chestnut tree.

Follow a footpath by the river for a little way, then turn left by a bench to the public road. Continue along the road until you see the main road (A96).

Just before the main road, turn right on to a grassy track which leads you under the road by the river.

If you want to enter Fochabers, you can do this by turning left on the main road, or by following the track which skirts the southern edge of the town.

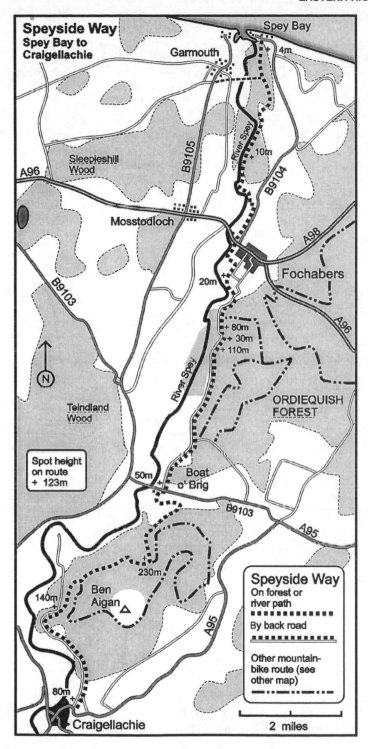

Speyside Way
Spey Bay to
Craigellachie

Spey Bay

Garmouth

+ 4m

River Spey

+ 10m

Sleepieshill
Wood

A96

B9105

B9104

Mosstodloch

A98

20m +

Fochabers

B9103

A96

+ 80m
+ 30m
+ 110m

River Spey

ORDIEQUISH
FOREST

N

Teindland
Wood

Spot height
on route
+ 123m

50m +

Boat
o' Brig

B9103

A95

230m

140m +

Ben
Aigan

A95

Speyside Way
On forest or
river path
▪▪▪▪▪▪▪▪▪▪▪▪▪
By back road
▬▬▬▬▬▬▬▬▬

Other mountain-
bike route (see
other map)
▪▬▪▬▪▬▪▬▪▬

80m +

Craigellachie

2 miles

FOCHABERS TO CRAIGELLACHIE
(13 miles)

Fochabers is an attractive small town with plenty of places to eat (Quaich Café, Tart and Pie Shop, and plenty of shops).

This section is hillier, particularly around Ben Aigan. After passing under the A96 on the grassy track (see previous section), keep by the river, then turn left before a little bridge. Cross a road, right to West Street, and rejoin the track by a school.

After this the trail gets a bit more technical on a bike. Filter left to avoid steps, and duck at the tree! There are a few more steps, and you eventually turn right on to a road.

After a climb pass Slorachs Wood. There is a scenic picnic spot on the opposite side of the road. One of the entry points to Forestry Commission mountain-bike routes is here.

After this there is a steep descent with a tight bend at the bottom, followed by a fierce climb. Following on there is a long descent, gradual at first, to Boat o' Brig, with fine views of the River Spey below.

At Boat o' Brig, cross the B9103 – this can be busy. Turn right, then immediately left up steps by a house with a portico to leave the public road.

Climbing steadily now, turn left at farm buildings, and follow an electricity line into the forest. Turn right uphill again at a gun-club sign.

The track dips into Ben Aigan Forest, then skirts it, giving good views of the Spey Valley. After this it enters the forest and climbs steeply to a forest road. Turn right here.

There is an initial drop, a further climb, then a fast descent to leave the forest at a mountain-biking sign. Turn left on to the public road and descend further; turn right at the A95 to enter Craigellachie.

The ranger's office is at Craigellachie (01340-881266). You can camp here free of charge at an attractive site by the river. There are toilets and washbasins with cold water only, and no other facilities. Craigellachie has a Spar food shop; there is also a friendly pub with a riverside garden and a good hotel.

THE SPEYSIDE WAY

Craigellachie to Ballindalloch

GENERAL NOTES

This part of the Speyside Way is entirely on the former Strathspey railway line, so the gradients are very easy. The way the railway engineers achieved this was to follow the river, so the views are pretty good too.

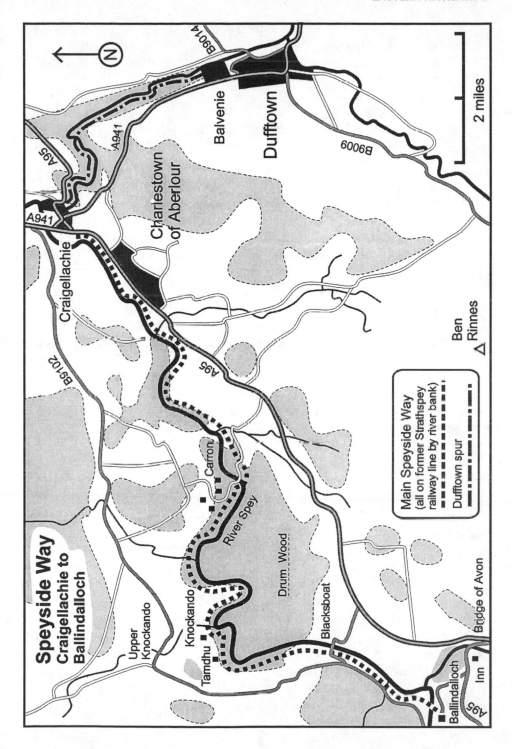

Speyside Way
Craigellachie to Ballindalloch

Main Speyside Way
(all on former Strathspey
railway line by river bank)

Dufftown spur

N

2 miles

B9014

Balvenie

Dufftown

B9009

Charlestown
of Aberlour

A941

A95

Craigellachie

A941

B9102

A95

Carron

River Spey

Ben
Rinnes

Drum Wood

Knockando

Blacksboat

Upper
Knockando

Tamdhu

Ballindalloch

Inn

Bridge of Avon

A95

This part of the route is studded with famous distilleries, all producing the smooth Speyside malt whisky. The dirt surface of the path is generally quite smooth; immediately south of Craigellachie there are some long grassy sections.

DUFFTOWN
SPUR
(4 miles)

Follow the old Strathspey railway line from Craigellachie to Dufftown up the valley of the River Fiddich; turn left from the ranger's office, and follow the path past the toilet block.

Horse-riders occasionally use this part of the Speyside Way, so you need to take care if you meet one. Only the rider of the horse can know if his particular animal is used to bikes or not. The best thing to do is just wait, so that the horse and rider can clearly see you. Trying to squeeze past on the narrow track is definitely the wrong thing to do.

The route ends in Balvenie, at a picnic area just outside the town; it is easy cycling and very pretty.

Dufftown has the Glenfiddich distillery; visitors are welcome and there is an audio-visual display – and you get a free dram afterwards. There is a resident pipe band in Dufftown which often plays for tourists in the evening. The tourist office is in a sort of mini castle in the middle of the town (01340-820501).

Balvenie Castle, the impressive thirteenth-century lair of 'Black' Comyn, is next to the Glenfiddich distillery. It was a noble residence for 400 years and was visited by Edward the First in 1304 and by Mary, Queen of Scots in 1562. This is still quite a large castle building, although the moat is now dried out. Admission is £1.20 (75p for concessions), or walk round outside for nothing in the evening.

There is also a museum in Dufftown with displays of local history. Also worth visiting is Mortlach Church, which has been in continual use for public worship since 566.

CRAIGELLACHIE TO
BALLINDALLOCH
(12 miles)

This section, on the old Strathspey railway line, is really lovely. There are striking views of the River Spey, and it's also surprisingly quiet. Being completely flat with no motor traffic, it's ideal for children.

In Craigellachie, by the ranger's office, turn right on to the old railway line (turning left takes you to Dufftown). The track bed runs under the main road, then follows the river bank. There is a small tunnel. Horses are allowed, although we never met any.

The route runs through a park in Aberlour. There is a tea room in the old station building run by ladies from the local church. If this isn't your scene, you can always go to the Station Bar.

After this the route rolls along by the river through mixed woodland. You pass the former halt of Dailuaine, cross a minor road, then cross the river on a combined 'rail'/road bridge. Turn left on to the path again.

The track runs by the Knockando and Tamdhu distilleries. You can see a copper still containing 3,180 gallons of malt whisky, just ten yards away from the path at Knockando. Visits are by arrangement only, but if you ask nicely they'll let you use the toilet. When we were checking out this route the lady at Tamdhu distillery offered us a free dram, but as it was 11 in the morning we declined, whereupon she kindly made us a cup of tea. This so overwhelmed Dave that he bought a bottle of the hard stuff – not that he needs much encouragement!

After Tamdhu the path runs high above the river, giving lovely views. There's a small viaduct with steps down. You pass under the B9102 at Blacksboat, where there are picnic tables, then you roll along by wide meanders in the river to the former railway bridge at Ballindalloch.

Cross the bridge to Ballindalloch Station, now a hostel (no resident warden; phone 01540-651272 to book in advance).

THE SPEYSIDE WAY

Ballindalloch to Glenlivet

GENERAL NOTES

This part of the Speyside Way is more challenging and is not suitable for young children. Towards the end of the route the walking and mountain-biking routes diverge.

The walking route takes you over a fragile upland area, while the mountain-biking route follows an old track further east. This is quite steep with a tricky descent.

BALLINDALLOCH
TO GLENLIVET
(8 miles)

This section begins on a road. Turn left on to the minor road by Ballindalloch Hostel; after a mile this joins the A95 at a T-junction, where you turn left. The A95 is reasonably quiet, but there is a rough track on the far side.

Follow the A95 for just under a mile, past a wee church and shop at Bridge of Avon, to the Delnashaugh Inn. If you don't mind slumming it with Range Rovers and BMWs this is a fairly grand place to have lunch.

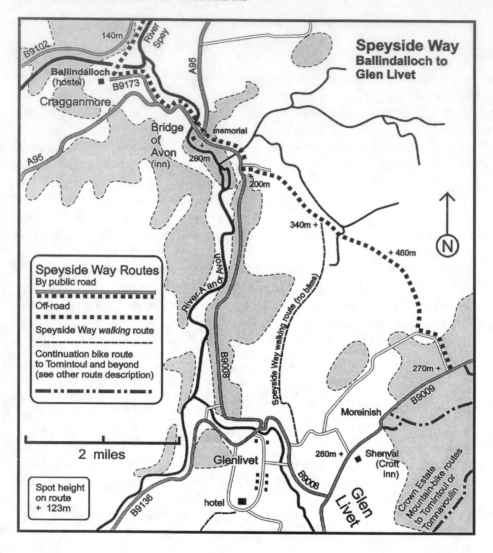

At the sharp bend in the road by the war memorial, turn right on to the B9008. Follow this for two-thirds of a mile, then at the foot of the hill turn left to a farm road to Auldich.

Pass under electricity pylons; shortly after this the farm road becomes a track. The walking route turns right off the track, but if you have a bike you are not allowed to go this way and should keep straight on up the hill.

Follow the track to the top of the hill. You cross a heathery grouse moor. There is a burn to ford, then there's a fast, bumpy descent on the other side where you meet a minor road again.

To go to the Croft Inn (see map), turn right at a white harled bungalow with a wood fence. There is a fast descent with fine views over Strathavon, then a brief climb. Turn left here to descend again to the inn on the B9009.

Alternatively, if you aren't in need of refreshment, bear left at the white harled bungalow; this takes you more directly to the B9009. Turn right on to the B9009 and after a mile you will see a forest entry point on your left-hand side. This gives access to signposted mountain-bike routes created by the Crown Estate.

If you went to the Croft Inn, turn south for Glenlivet or turn north on the B9009 to the forest entry at Morinish for the off-road route south.

It's quite straightforward to cycle on quiet roads to Tomintoul from here. They are very hilly but they have great views.

You should not attempt to bike the Speyside Way walking route between Glenlivet and Tomintoul. Instead there are a number of dedicated off-road bike routes created by the Crown Estate – see Glenlivet Mountain-Bike Trails.

The distillery at Glenlivet offers the usual free tour and free dram, but it also has a coffee shop (although you have to pay for coffee!).

USEFUL CONTACTS

The Speyside Way ranger station at Craigellachie is manned during the summer and you can phone them on 01340-881266. If you are sitting at home in the winter you can still get information by contacting Moray Council, Leisure Department, High Street, Elgin; 01343-545121.

For general information about the area, or to make B&B reservations in advance, contact Moray Tourist Board, 17 High Street, Elgin; 01343-543388.

There are banks at Fochabers, Rothes, Dufftown, Aberlour and Tomintoul. If you want to hire a bike there is a mountain-bike hirer at Craigellachie (01340-881525).

SPEY VALLEY FORESTS

Varied forest bike rides between Fochabers and Craigellachie.

GENERAL NOTES

This area is 50 miles east of Inverness. Mass tourism is mainly limited to the whisky-trail circuit. Outdoor activities here include salmon-fishing, golf, hillwalking and, more recently, mountain-biking. The area is particularly suited to mountain-biking, as the routes here are quite varied and have some good views. The Ben Aigan routes are the most difficult. All the routes can easily be interconnected. Ordiequish and Ben Aigan Forests are best linked by part of the long-distance Speyside Way, a bikeable off-road trail north to Spey Bay and south as far as Ballindalloch.

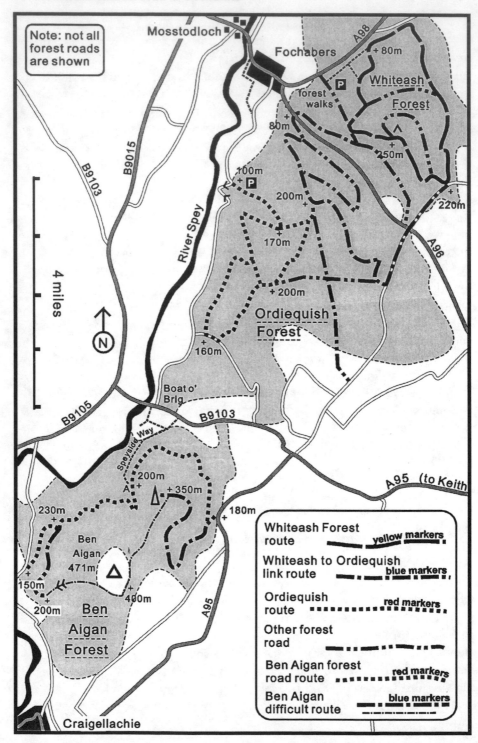

Note: not all forest roads are shown

Mosstodloch

Fochabers

+ 80m

Whiteash

Forest

Torest walks

+ 80m

+ 250m

B9015

B9103

River Spey

+ 100m

+ 200m

+ 170m

+ 220m

+ 200m

A96

A98

Ordiequish

Forest

+ 160m

Boat o' Brig

B9105

B9103

Speyside Way

+ 200m

+ 350m

+ 230m

+ 180m

Ben Aigan 471m

+ 150m

+ 400m

+ 200m

Ben

Aigan

Forest

A95

A95 (to Keith

4 miles

N

Whiteash Forest route — yellow markers

Whiteash to Ordiequish link route — blue markers

Ordiequish route — red markers

Other forest road

Ben Aigan forest road route — red markers

Ben Aigan difficult route — blue markers

Craigellachie

WHITEASH AND ORDIEQUISH FORESTS

WHITEASH FOREST ROUTE
(8 miles)

Just east of Fochabers, Whiteash Forest is only moderately hilly. All of the route is on forest roads. The western side of the forest, around the forest walks area, is the most varied, with Scots pine, birch and mixed spruce. The south and east is more uniform plantation forest. There are some good views, particularly from the Duchess of Richmond Monument.

Walking and mountain-bike routes are both signposted; the mountain-bike routes have the usual colour-coded sign, and the walking routes are marked with blue triangles. Strictly speaking, you should dismount if you stray on to these; this is worth doing, as they are quite scenic.

Fochabers has a choice of tea rooms and pubs; the most convenient tea room for this route is in a garden centre near the junction of the A96 and A98.

WHITEASH TO ORDIEQUISH LINK ROUTE
(6 miles)

This is the most interesting route, both scenically and technically. Starting from Whiteash there is a gentle climb, then a fast descent to the A96. Take care crossing.

After this there is a steady climb through mixed woodland in Slorach's Wood. This leads to a fast descent to the minor road which forms the east boundary of Ordiequish Forest. Return to Whiteash is on this road, crossing the A96 again at a sign saying 'Braes of Enzie'.

ORDIEQUISH ROUTE
(5.5 miles)

To join this route from Fochabers, start from East Main Street, then join Ordiequish Road to bike south on the minor road just east of the River Spey. After two miles turn left, following the mountain-bike sign.

After a short distance you pass a small car park, then there is a steady climb to a T-junction, where you turn right. There are a few turn-offs which are not signposted; ignore these. The path becomes bumpy, then turns into a grassy track; shortly after this it joins a minor road. Turn left here, then, after 300 metres, turn left again into the forest.

After two miles you have the choice of turning left to return to the start or turning right to join the blue route.

BEN AIGAN FOREST

Connecting Ordiequish to Ben Aigan Forest is best done via the Speyside Way. Join the minor road just east of the River Spey and bike south. There is a steep descent and a very steep climb just after the Ordiequish entry, followed by a gentle descent which eventually plunges to Boat o' Brig.

At Boat o' Brig cross the B9103, then turn right. Immediately after, turn left up some steps by a house with a portico to leave the public road. Turn left at farm buildings and follow an electricity line into the forest. Turn right at a gun-club sign. This track joins the Ben Aigan red route at the point marked 'A' on the map.

BEN AIGAN
RED ROUTE
(5 miles)

This is entirely on forest roads but is quite hilly, particularly so at the start and finish, where there is a steep descent to the public road. There are good views over the Spey Valley; the west end of the route forms part of the Speyside Way.

BEN AIGAN
BLUE ROUTE
(6 miles)

The greater part of this route is along a rough track, not a forest road; it is best done east to west as the steep descent west of Ben Aigan would not be bikeable in an uphill direction. The logical approach to Ben Aigan is to do the whole red/blue circuit in a clockwise direction.

Riders who went over this route commented that the off-road sections were only just bikeable, but the views were superb. The route skirts an area of open hillside at the top of the hill; following this there is a very steep descent over half a mile of rough track. This joins a forest road with more gentle gradients.

There is an attractive pub with a beer garden by the river in Craigellachie.

AROUND LOCH MUICK

A gentle cycle round about the loch, or a much more serious route which would take all day.

GENERAL NOTES

Just south of Balmoral Castle and quite near Ballater is the shapely mountain of Lochnagar and beautiful Loch Muick. Loch Muick is a typical Cairngorm loch, its basin scoured out of rock by glaciers.

Loch Muick is best seen on a cold winter's day, with a gale blowing down the loch and snow threatening. Then you get a true sense of its remote beauty. It's not quite the same on a warm Sunday, with cars parked along the road to the glen and sun-loungers all along the roadside.

I was told by a friend who knows the area that this explosion of people by the roadside was due to Prince Charles publicising the estate in a television programme. I don't know if this is true or not, but the local ranger asked me

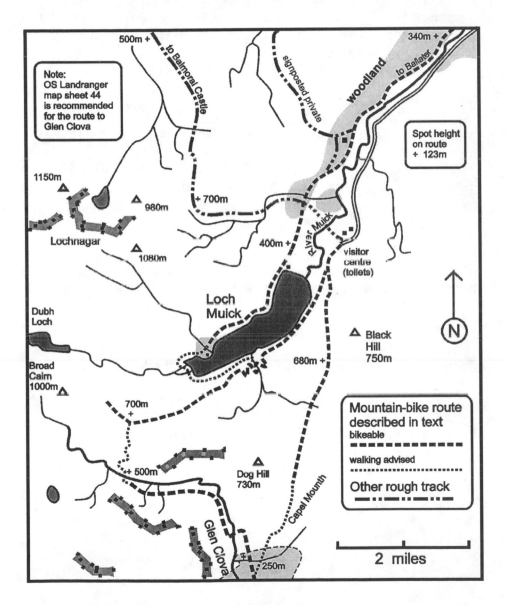

how I would feel if cars were banned from the glen and a shuttle bus provided instead. Naturally I was in favour of this idea.

In any case, you don't have to bike up the glen road, as there is a dirt track on the other side of the river.

Loch Muick
(6 miles round loch)

You can bike much of the way round the loch, but you should walk rather than bike on the footpath section. The house in trees on the north shore was once owned by Queen Victoria.

There are some easy tracks at the east end of the loch.

Loch Muick to Glen Clova and Return
(16 miles)

This is an all-day route (dotted line on map). It involves a considerable amount of ascent, first to get out of Glen Muick, then another steep climb to get out of Glen Clova.

The greater part of the route is on Land Rover tracks. The part that isn't, the descent into Glen Clova and the climb out of it, will involve you getting off your bike.

It's best to do it clockwise, if only for the great views over Loch Muick on the return leg. A proper map and compass and warm, waterproof clothing are essential.

Other Options

The track which runs north-west from Loch Muick by way of Lochnagar is shown on some maps as being a footpath for part of the way. In fact it's a steep Land Rover track.

At the north end it finishes near Balmoral Castle, summer residence of the Queen. People do go this way, although the factor of Balmoral Estate is said not to like mountain-bikes. What the Queen might think about it is uncertain; however, she is patron of the Cyclists' Touring Club.

The track shown on the north-west side of the River Muick is a gentle descent all the way to the B976 near Ballater.

Access from the Ballater end is a mile west of the signposted road leading up the glen. There is a post box at this junction, and, a little further up, a sign to deter cars: locked deer gate. Not a problem for bikes, though, although in fact, when we cycled up the track, we found that the sign was untrue and there wasn't a locked gate at all.

LOCAL FACILITIES

There used to be a SYHA youth hostel in Ballater, but unfortunately this closed several years ago. The nearest hostel by road is now in Braemar. The nearest actual hostel is in Glen Doll, which is a side glen off Glen Clova. To get to this you would, of course, need to be doing the mountain-bike route to Glen Clova.

There is a good choice of B&Bs, hotels and eating places in Ballater; there is also a bike shop and tourist office (01339-755306). The visitor centre at Loch Muick has an information display but no other facilities apart from toilets.

GLEN TANAR AND MOUNT KEEN

Easy routes in the forest, a more difficult route, or a very difficult route!

GENERAL NOTES

Glen Tanar is one of a number of side valleys of the River Dee where remnants of the ancient Wood of Caledon are preserved.

There are three suggestions here: a moderately difficult route via the Black Moss; a long, difficult route via Mount Keen to Glen Esk; or simply exploring the forest tracks in the Caledonian pine forest.

An important part of the preservation of this type of forest is that old trees are allowed to be blown over in storms, so exposing open soil for seedlings to germinate. This will only occur successfully where seedlings are protected from deer and sheep. This is why gates should be shut and deer fences not climbed over except where stiles are provided.

BLACK MOSS ROUTE
(17 miles circular)

Start at Tombae on the B976; this is opposite the junction of the A97 and A93 on the other side of the River Dee.

The track passes a farm (height 200 metres) and climbs south-west, rising steeply at times. The ascent is continuous with a fairly bumpy surface. There are good views behind you, of Loch Kinord across the Dee, so stop and have a look occasionally.

There is a shallow descent across Black Moss, then another steep climb to 540 metres. At this point Mount Keen and Glen Tanar become visible.

A fast descent follows; this is difficult in places owing to water erosion but is still bikeable.

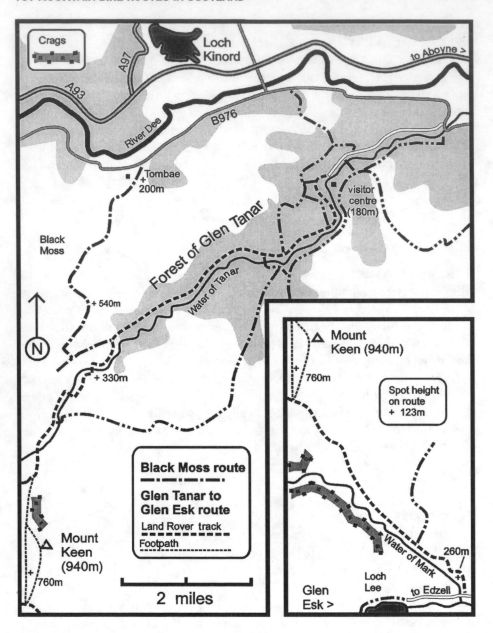

At the foot of the hill, turn left at a T-junction to go down the glen. A mile after this there is another junction nearer the river; continue down the glen towards the trees.

This is a gradual descent, sometimes with gravel and sand surfaces; return to Tombae on the B976.

BIKING IN THE FOREST

Glen Tanar is south-west of Aboyne off the A93. Follow the B976 south of the River Dee. The Glen Tanar road starts by a bridge with an adjacent tower and is clearly signposted.

Continue up, passing a forest car park, then on to a set of farm buildings in Scottish baronial style. Turn right here following the right-of-way sign round the farm. Pass a sign saying 'Ca Canny Doon the Brae', and you are in the forest.

The most interesting ride is to follow the track going up the glen by the side of the Water of Tanar.

There is little danger of getting lost in the forest, as returning to the river will take you to the exit. If you meet any horse-riders, stop to let them pass.

MOUNT KEEN TO GLEN ESK

(16 miles off-road)

This is a hard ride with a lot of climbing. Warm, waterproof clothing, a 1:50,000 OS map and a compass are essential. Don't forget to take enough food. The top section may involve some walking.

Start in the forest as before but continue up the Water of Tanar to where the glen becomes steep-sided and narrow. At this point turn south towards Mount Keen, crossing the burn.

The track continues for a little further, then curves round to the west. Leave it here and take the footpath towards the summit, passing to the west of some crags. You will probably have to walk here, as it is quite rocky.

After a further climb the path branches in two, the left fork leading to the summit of the mountain. Take the right fork; this section is just bikeable, and is a gentle ascent, a flat section, then a gradual descent to a track leading into Glen Mark.

Descend down Glen Mark to the public road in Glen Esk.

LOCAL FACILITIES

Unfortunately the youth hostel in Ballater closed in 1995. The best option now is The Wolf's Hearth, Tornaveen, by Banchory, 01339-883460 (not SYHA). There are tourist information offices at Aboyne (01339-886060) and Ballater (01339-755306).

There are plenty of pubs and tea rooms in Aboyne, which is quite near the foot of Glen Tanar. On the other side, at Glen Esk, there is a tea room halfway down the glen and lots of eating places, plus B&Bs and hotels in Edzell.

Fetteresso and Drumtochty

A wide choice of routes in these forests near Stonehaven.

General Notes

These two forests are inside a triangle created by the River Dee to the north, the Water of Dye to the west, and the A94 Dundee to Aberdeen road to the south. If you are getting there using the A94, bear in mind that access from the dual carriageway is restricted at some junctions.

The hills here are rolling rather than mountainous, but there are still some great views over this Grassic Gibbon country.

All the mountain-biking is on forest roads. There is often a climb to start with, but after that the routes aren't particularly hilly.

This is a good area for children, as the routes are quite extensive but still easy enough for them to bike considerable distances.

As usual the trees are mostly spruce, but recent felling in some areas means you aren't hemmed in all the time. There is more variety of trees in the lower sections, with the area around Drumtochty Glen being particularly pretty.

There are plenty of forest roads which don't form part of the bike routes. There is no reason why you shouldn't bike on these too; the only trouble is you might get lost. A map is useless if you're surrounded by trees and don't know where you are!

The minor roads in the area between Auchenblae and Stonehaven are fairly quiet and have good views.

Yellow Route
(7 miles, circular)

This is reached from the A957 Slug Road running between Crathes in Deeside and Stonehaven. There is a bit of a climb to start with, but after that the hills are easier. At its western end it meets the white route which links the two forests.

Blue Route
(9 miles, circular)

This starts from the Forestry Commission car park at Quithel. This is off the minor road between Auchenblae and Stonehaven.

This time there is a longer climb from the car park, but again once you are up there the gradients are fairly easy. There are some fine views over the Mearns countryside towards the North Sea on the southern parts.

There is also a linking route with white markers leading to the car park at Swanley. You can avoid some of the climb up by going that way, although it's a bit longer.

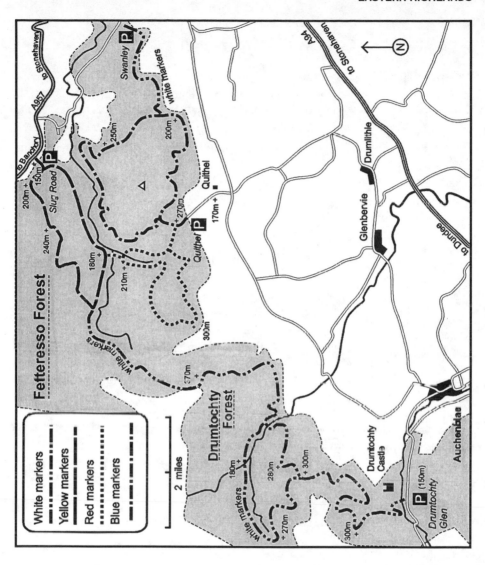

RED ROUTE

(6 miles, circular)

This is very similar to the blue route but slightly shorter, if a wee bit hillier. It begins from the same point, the Quithel car park. Some parts of the route are likely to be muddy if it's been wet.

WHITE ROUTE

(Loop 7 miles)
(Link to car park 5 miles)
(Link to yellow route 5 miles)

This is the most interesting of the routes, as it twists and turns in the lower sections near Drumtochty Castle. There are some steep sections but these are mostly fairly short.

The link to the yellow route includes some good views over the Mearns and surrounding areas.

This is the only route which is reasonably close to a pub. For this reason, if you plan to bike over all the routes, you might like to start and finish in Auchenblae.

LOCAL FACILITIES

Just east of the routes is the former fishing port of Stonehaven. This has a big choice of tea rooms, B&Bs and hotels. There is a tourist information office (01569-762806).

The village of Auchenblae, fairly close to the white route, is pretty, with steep, winding streets. It has two pubs/ hotels and a food shop.

I met the former owner of Drumtochty Castle in the pub here. He seemed quite pleased to be out of it and now lives in the village. The castle isn't open to the public. If you like visiting castles as well as mountain-biking, however, the best one to visit in the area is definitely Dunnottar Castle; this is just south of Stonehaven.

There is no pub or hotel in Glenbervie, but there is a hotel in Drumlithie. If you are looking for a restaurant there is a good one at Clatterin' Brig. This is just off my map, where the minor road leading through Drumtochty Glen meets the B974.

GLEN ISLA TO GLEN PROSEN

A demanding mountain-bike route in the Angus Glens.

INTRODUCTION

The route starts in forest in Glen Isla, then climbs up Glen Finlet and crosses to Glen Prosen. A short section must be walked.

Return to the start is via Glen Uig. Anyone who has children, or who wants an easier day, could explore the forest trails at the start of the route.

FREUCHIES TO GLEN FINLET

(7 miles)

Start on the B951 just east of Kirkton of Glenisla (just off map). To get to this

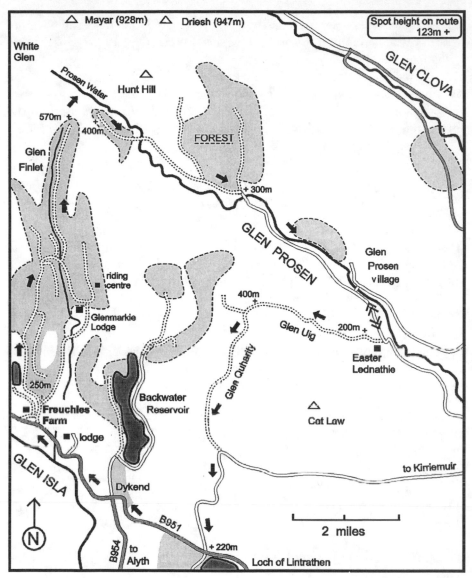

△ Mayar (928m)   △ Driesh (947m)

Spot height on route
123m +

White
Glen

Prosen Water

△
Hunt Hill

570m +

400m +

FOREST

Glen
Finlet

+ 300m

GLEN CLOVA

GLEN PROSEN

Glen
Prosen
village

riding
centre

400m +

Glen Uig

200m +

Glenmarkie
Lodge

Glen Quharity

Easter
Lednathie

250m

Backwater
Reservoir

△
Cat Law

Freuchies
Farm

lodge

to Kirriemuir

GLEN ISLA

Dykend

N

B954

B951

to
Alyth

+ 220m

Loch of Lintrathen

2 miles

from the south, go through Blairgowrie to Alyth. After this follow signs for Glen
Isla. The start of the route is a short distance after a lodge (Highland Adventure
Outdoor Centre) and is signposted Glenmarkie Farm Riding Centre.

Follow the track and bear right over the river. At a small car park with a cross-
country-skiing route map, turn left into the forest. Climb past Loch Shandra,
with open hillside to the left.

As the climb steepens you approach a white cottage, then you enter the forest
again. The trail gradually levels off, and you meet a crossroads. If you are not
doing the full route you could explore here, otherwise keep straight on.

The route sweeps round to the east, descending rapidly to a small concrete bridge. Immediately after the bridge turn sharp left up Glen Finlet, where there is a gentle climb.

Keep right on to the end of the track in Glen Finlet, passing an end-of-trail sign for skiers. It ends in a small glade with a burn running through.

Dismount and push your bike, following the small burn to the edge of the forest. You will need to cross the burn at several points, but this is not difficult. Climb over the stile to open hillside.

GLEN FINLET TO GLEN ISLA

(24 miles, via Glen Prosen)

At the sign erected by the Scottish Rights of Way Society, turn right and push your bike uphill, keeping the deer fence on your right-hand side. After a little way, when you see the Col (high pass), climb over it to descend to Glen Prosen.

This part is not bikeable, but after you have descended for a few hundred metres the rocky hillside gives way to mixed grass and heather, which you may be able to ride down.

Go straight down the hill to the river (Prosen Water), the high corrie of White Glen to the left. At the river follow the right bank downstream. A grassy surface gives way to a Land Rover track. Eventually you encounter a big steel gate; go through this to a forest road.

Go down this fast, bumpy track, crossing the river to the public road at Glenprosen Lodge. A sign here gives notice of deer-stalking periods; access to the hills may be restricted at certain times (12 August to 20 October is best avoided).

Continue down the public road, keeping to the right bank of the river. A left turn over a bridge leads to Glen Prosen village, which has a tea room. Keep on the west bank of the river, following signs for Lednathie and Pearsie.

After passing Glen Prosen village there is a very steep uphill climb, followed by a shorter descent. At a sharp left bend in the public road, turn right for Glen Uig, signposted Wester Lednathie.

There is a very hilly section, then the road becomes a track. Shortly after this there is a fork in the track; take the left fork and descend to the burn, the deep 'V' of the pass ahead. There is a crow trap at the top of the pass. Turn left here to a grassy track, passing through a wooden gate. Ignore the other path which climbs steeply up a hill.

This section is bikeable but requires care. After a few miles and a splash across a burn the track meets a minor road. Turn right on to the minor road and keep on going south until you meet the B951 just north of the Loch of Lintrathen.

Turn right, following the sign for Glen Isla. At the next crossroads, at Dykend, keep straight on to return to the start.

PLACES TO STAY

Highland Adventure (interesting lodge): 01575-582238; tourist information: 01575-574097.

PUBS AND TEA ROOMS

You could try The Singing Kettle at Alyth; there are also two hotels and a shop at Kirkton of Glenisla, a tea room in Glen Prosen village, and a tea room and craft shop at Peel Farm, south of the Loch of Lintrathen.

WESTERN HIGHLANDS

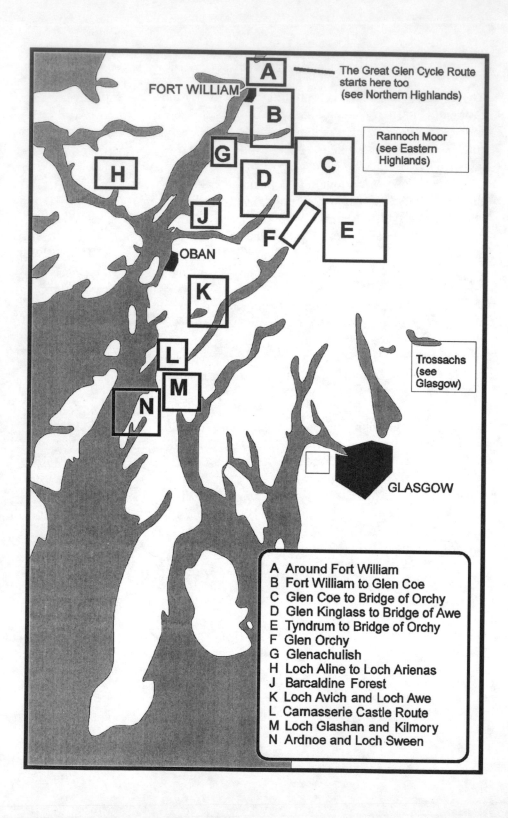

The Great Glen Cycle Route starts here too (see Northern Highlands)

FORT WILLIAM

Rannoch Moor (see Eastern Highlands)

OBAN

Trossachs (see Glasgow)

GLASGOW

A Around Fort William
B Fort William to Glen Coe
C Glen Coe to Bridge of Orchy
D Glen Kinglass to Bridge of Awe
E Tyndrum to Bridge of Orchy
F Glen Orchy
G Glenachulish
H Loch Aline to Loch Arienas
J Barcaldine Forest
K Loch Avich and Loch Awe
L Carnasserie Castle Route
M Loch Glashan and Kilmory
N Ardnoe and Loch Sween

OVERVIEW

The Western Highlands certainly has some of the most dramatic scenery in Scotland, and there's a considerable variety of top-quality mountain-biking as well. No matter what you're looking for, it's probably here: technically difficult routes in the big mountains, a gentle pootle round with the kids, or even a longer-distance route which could last several days.

The backbone of the long-distance route in this area is the northern part of the West Highland Way. Mountain-biking is not allowed on the West Highland Way south of Tyndrum, but north of this it's perfectly acceptable to mountain-bike it, apart from a couple of quite short bits that are described in the route guide.

Of course, the West Highland Way is possibly the most popular long-distance walk in Britain, so you'll meet walkers all along it. Courtesy is necessary if acceptable relations between walkers and mountain-bikers are to be maintained; failing that mountain-bikers will certainly be the losers.

You'd certainly meet far fewer walkers if you avoided the peak season and went in May or September – and fewer midges too! Some parts of The Way that can be used by mountain-bikes are also used for the Scottish Motorcycle Trials during late April/early May.

The West Highland Way is routes B, C and E in the diagram opposite. If you are mountain-biking it you can extend your route into Glen Orchy (route F in diagram), Glen Kinglass (route D), Rannoch Moor (described in Eastern Highlands), or The Great Glen Cycle Route (described in Northern Highlands).

Perhaps you aren't planning a mammoth mountain-bike trip, though; maybe what you'd like is a shorter route with good views of the lochs and mountains. The other routes in this area offer plenty of choice; most of them are near the coast and they've great views of the Western Isles and the sea lochs.

These routes are all maintained by the Forestry Commission and are marked out with colour-coded posts. The variety of trees is sometimes a bit limited, but in general the scenery is so interesting that this hardly matters. Most of these routes are quite varied, with steep sections in some that can be fast and exciting, and other routes that are fairly easy. The only exception to this are the routes in Glenachulish (route G), which are mostly pretty steep.

Around Fort William

A wide range of off-road biking near Fort William.

Most routes are easy; also technical mountain-bike routes in Leanachan Forest.

Leanachan Forest

Lying in the shadow of Ben Nevis and Aonach Mor, Leanachan Forest offers varied mountain-bike routes and the occasional spectacular view.

Most of the routes are signposted with wooden marker posts, colour-coded according to difficulty. This plantation forest consists of larch and spruce, with birch planted in the more public areas.

Most routes are graded easy (green), these being mainly on forest roads. Two minor roads from Torlundy and Leanachan are also used.

The higher signposted routes are more difficult, and there are tracks further up the mountain that are even more difficult. These are not signposted. Most difficult of all is the steep track descending to the distillery near Fort William.

Glen Loy

The routes in Glen Loy are not signposted, but it's quite easy to find your way around; all are on forest roads.

To bike between Leanachan and Glen Loy use the Caledonian Canal towpath, the B8004 and the A82; cross the canal at Moy using the swing bridge. This is manned between May and October, from 8 a.m. to 11 p.m. There is no way to cross the River Lochy from the minor road to the east.

Great Glen Cycle Route
(Caledonian Canal Towpath)

The Great Glen Cycle Route runs from Fort William to Inverness. The section shown on the map here is on a towpath and is a pleasant flat ride suitable for children. After Gairlochy the Great Glen Cycle Route uses the B8005, then forest tracks in Clunes Forest west of Loch Lochy.

The towpath section near Fort William could be linked to the B8004 to form a return route. The B8004 is quite hilly but has very good views.

Another alternative would be to return via Spean Bridge, using the minor road by the River Lochy. This is quite quiet, although the northern part is hilly. Some cycling on the A82 is unavoidable; the A82 is busy and quite narrow, so this should be kept to a minimum.

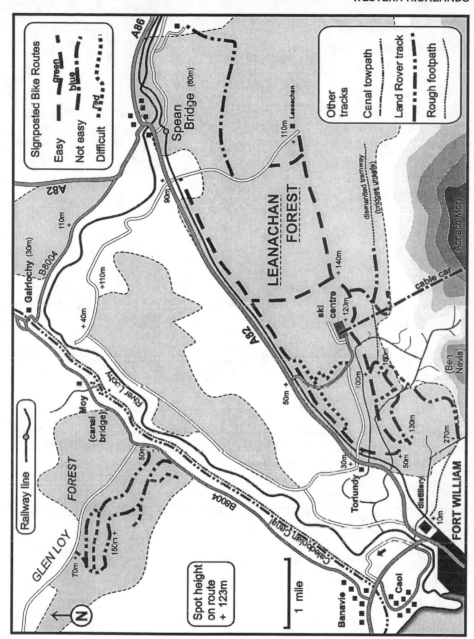

TEA ROOMS ETC.

There is the Stable Tea Room at Gairlochy and a choice of pubs and cafés, plus the Smiddy House Bistro in Spean Bridge. There is plenty of choice in Fort William; the outdoor shop Nevisport has a restaurant which is self-service and good value.

BIKE REPAIRS/BIKE HIRE

Off-beat Bikes, 117 High Street, Fort William; 01397-704008.

FORT WILLIAM TO GLEN COE

This route uses part of the West Highland Way, plus the occasional minor road. Spectacular scenery!

From Glen Coe you can continue south towards Oban or Tyndrum, nearly all of it off-road.

While the south part of the West Highland Way is not bikeable, parts of it north of Tyndrum can be cycled over. In this section the footpath between Glen Nevis and Lochan Lunn Da Bhra should be avoided on a bike; a minor road is used instead. In addition there is a section of very steep footpath near Kinlochleven to avoid; go by Mamore Lodge instead.

Please note that even if you feel able technically to cycle footpath sections, you still should not do this: biking causes damage to the path. Use the alternatives given here.

FORT WILLIAM TO LOCHAN LUNN DA BHRA
(5 miles)

This first section is on a minor road which climbs steeply out of Fort William; this has walking access at the south end of the High Street, signposted Upper Achintore. Alternatively reach this from the roundabout at the south end of the dual carriageway section of the A82, signposted Upper Achintore.

The road climbs out of Fort William, giving intermittent views of Loch Linnhe. There are several ups and downs, and after four miles you will see plantation forest on the left. When the Lochan comes into view, at a right bend, turn left through a gate to join a forest track.

LOCHAN LUNN DA BHRA TO MAMORE LODGE
(7 miles)

The first mile is in forest and is a steady climb. Then turn east to pass under the peaks of Stob Bann and Am Bodach. The path is bikeable, with some difficult sections and a number of burns to splash through.

Just after a ruined cottage at Tigh-na-sleubhaich you reach the summit of the path at 330 metres. After this there is a fast descent, gradually becoming steeper. At the end of this do not take the right-hand turn to the West Highland Way footpath, but continue straight on to Mamore Lodge.

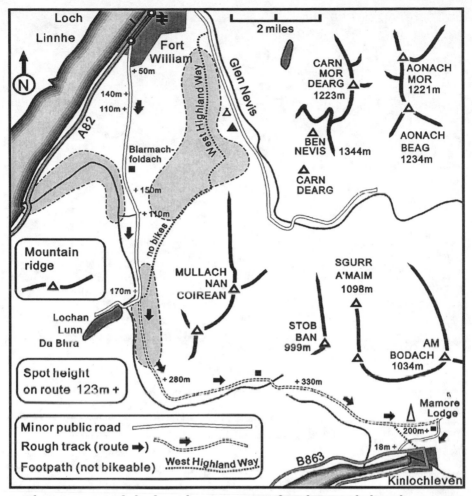

Loch Linnhe

Fort William
+ 50m

2 miles

CARN MOR DEARG 1223m

AONACH MOR 1221m

140m +
110m +

A82

Glen Nevis

West Highland Way

BEN NEVIS 1344m

AONACH BEAG 1234m

Blarmach-foldach

+ 150m

+ 110m

CARN DEARG

no bikes

Mountain ridge

170m +

MULLACH NAN COIREAN

SGURR A'MAIM 1098m

Lochan Lunn Da Bhra

STOB BAN 999m

AM BODACH 1034m

Spot height on route 123m +

+ 280m

+ 330m

Mamore Lodge
200m+

Minor public road

Rough track (route ➡)

18m +

Footpath (not bikeable) West Highland Way

B863

Kinlochleven

There is an initial climb, with a great view of Loch Leven below, then a steep plunge past a radio mast. At the bottom, bear right to the hotel (01855-831213).

Historic Mamore Lodge is the best place to stay in Kinlochleven; it certainly has the best view. The hotel also has an economical bunkhouse and can provide excellent bar lunches. If you are doing the trip as a day excursion from Fort William and intend to return the way you came, it's probably best not to descend the further 200 metres into Kinlochleven.

MAMORE LODGE TO GLEN COE

(10 miles to youth hostel)

The walking route between Kinlochleven and Glen Coe goes by way of The Devil's Staircase; this is a very steep footpath and not recommended.

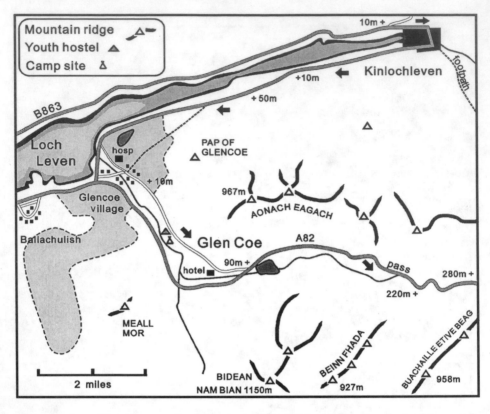

Nevertheless, I have seen competition-standard riders bike the whole thing, and it was recently featured as a mountain-bike route in a well-known magazine (travelling south to north).

The route described here is all on-road, but it is included so that this route can be linked to the West Highland Way between the Kingshouse Hotel (Glen Coe) and Bridge of Orchy. Further extensions off-road can be made into Glen Kinglass (to Oban), into Auch Gleann, or to Tyndrum.

There is a surfaced road from Mamore Lodge to the B863 by Loch Leven, but it is extremely steep, with few passing places and lots of blind corners.

After Kinlochleven, cycle along the B863 to Glencoe village, then take the minor road on the east side of the River Coe. There are various accommodation options here; the hostel is attractive, but advance booking is best. Just beyond is the Red Squirrel Camp Site, in an attractive situation by the River Coe (but may be midge-infested). A mile beyond this is the Clachaig Hotel. Camping is possible near here, and is convenient for the pub, too.

If you are intending to continue east through the Pass of Glencoe it is suggested you stay overnight at the foot of the glen. Go through the pass in the early morning when there is less traffic and the light in the glen is best. Some of the public road in the glen can be avoided by using the old road which is now a rough track.

GLEN COE TO BRIDGE OF ORCHY

Off-road by Rannoch Moor and the Blackmount Mountains.

GENERAL NOTES

This route is described travelling south, to link with other routes. Walkers will mostly be going in the opposite direction, so will see you in good time. Take warm, waterproof clothing.

The route starts at the Kingshouse Hotel in Glen Coe. This is much frequented by climbers. Wild camping is allowed behind the hotel; there is also a youth hostel and a campsite with facilities ten miles further west at the foot of Glen Coe.

KINGSHOUSE HOTEL TO VICTORIA BRIDGE
(9 miles)

Take the track which leads south-east from the car park at the front of the hotel. After a mile, carefully cross the A82, following the White Corries sign. After a short distance, fork left opposite Black Rock Cottage. This much-photographed building is owned by the Scottish Ladies Climbing Club; the impressive ramparts of Buachaille Etive Mor behind make a fine setting.

The track climbs south-east as it skirts the hill Meall a Bhuridh leaving the Glen Coe Ski Centre. After a couple of miles it levels off and turns south towards the Black Mount. There is a continuous descent to the Ba Bridge.

The source of the River Ba is a lochan three miles to the west in a hanging valley 1,000 feet above Corrie Ba. Loch Ba is two miles to the east. The old bridge with its cascading waterfalls is a fine place for a picnic.

The rough track, which mostly follows the line of a General Wade road, presents no problems to a mountain-biker. You're virtually certain to meet walkers coming in the opposite direction; a friendly word as you pass is a good idea.

After Ba Bridge there is a gradual climb as the path skirts the Stob Chabhar range. By the time you begin the descent to Loch Tulla you are on a well-compacted stony surface. Try to keep to the main path rather than riding to the side of it, which will lead to erosion.

There is a fast descent passing woods of natural Scots pine, and Loch Tulla comes into view; the big mountain on the far side is Ben Dorian. The track finally ends at Victoria Bridge.

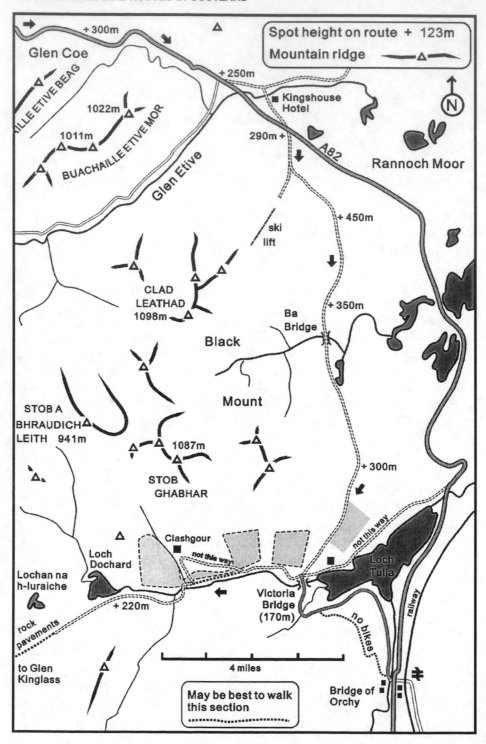

Spot height on route + 123m
Mountain ridge ——————△——

Glen Coe

+ 300m

AILLE ETIVE BEAG

1022m

1011m

BUACHAILLE ETIVE MOR

Glen Etive

+ 250m

Kingshouse Hotel

290m +

A82

Rannoch Moor

ski lift

+ 450m

CLAD LEATHAD 1098m

Ba Bridge

+ 350m

Black

Mount

STOB A BHRAUDICH LEITH   941m

1087m

STOB GHABHAR

+ 300m

not this way

Loch Dochard

Clashgour

not this way

Loch Tulla

Lochan na h-Iuraiche

rock pavements

+ 220m

Victoria Bridge (170m)

no bikes

railway

to Glen Kinglass

4 miles

Bridge of Orchy

May be best to walk this section

VICTORIA BRIDGE TO BRIDGE OF ORCHY
(4 miles)

On the north side of the river another path leads off to the west, signposted Public Footpath to Loch Etive via Glen Kinglass. It is possible to bike this way (see next section). The private road leading to the east leads to Black Mount Lodge. The estate, one of the most beautiful in Scotland, was once owned by Ian Fleming, creator of James Bond/007. After the death of Ian Fleming it remained in the family, passing to his brother.

The road on the far side of Victoria Bridge is the A8005. Despite its classification, this is a single-track road with passing places; it is quiet. The West Highland Way follows it for half a mile to the Inveroran Hotel, then turns south following a track over the hill of Mam Carraigh. Bikes should not be taken on this section; use the road.

The Inveroran Hotel is, to my mind, preferable to the Bridge of Orchy Hotel, even if it lacks some of its facilities. They serve generous bar meals to travellers on the West Highland Way. At the time of writing, wild camping was allowed by the bridge west of the hotel; however, numbers are gradually increasing, and the lack of toilet facilities may force the estate to introduce a small campsite. The Bridge of Orchy Hotel incorporates a bunkhouse, which is another option.

VICTORIA BRIDGE TO GLEN KINGLASS

It is possible to mountain-bike from Victoria Bridge into Glen Kinglass and eventually to Loch Etive. A dirt road leads south from there all the way to Bridge of Awe. This is only 15 miles by public road from Oban. This route is more difficult. For the section beyond Lochan na h-luraiche (see map), refer to the next route.

From Victoria Bridge travel west, following the sign for Glen Kinglass/Loch Etive. At the second patch of forest, shortly after a climbing-club hut, fork left off the Land Rover track and follow the footpath by the river. Until recently it was possible for cyclists to continue along to Clashgour; however, an out-of-control mountain-biker crashed into the shepherd's car as his wife was fetching the children from school, so it's now advisable to use the path.

Going by the river is very beautiful but you will have to walk in places. It rejoins the track south of Clashgour, after which there is a river crossing (stepping stones). Do not cross if the river is high. After this the track becomes rougher, but still bikeable. After the summit of the path the route descends over rock pavements to Glen Kinglass.

GLEN KINGLASS TO BRIDGE OF AWE

A remote bike route which involves a river crossing and some rougher sections – and great scenery!

GENERAL NOTES

As mentioned above, it is possible to mountain-bike from Victoria Bridge (near Bridge of Orchy) into Glen Kinglass and eventually to Loch Etive. A dirt road leads south from there all the way to Bridge of Awe. Bridge of Awe is 15 miles by public road from Oban. This route is quite difficult, and the section by Loch Etive is very hilly. For the route east of Lochan na h-luraiche (see map), refer to the previous route. Mountain-bikers are asked to note that they should avoid the Land Rover track to Clashgour, east of Lochan na h-luraiche (just off the map); use the public footpath to the south instead, keeping by the river all the time.

GLEN KINGLASS TO LOCH ETIVE

(10 miles Lochan na h-luraiche to Loch Etive)

As mentioned, entry to Glen Kinglass from the east is from Victoria Bridge. After the summit of the pass the route descends over rock pavements to Glen Kinglass. Cross the narrow footbridge over the river – you will probably have to carry your bike – and continue south-west on the north bank of the river. At first there isn't any path, but if you continue downstream you'll soon pick it up.

Once you find the path, the next challenge is to bike it. Experienced mountain-bikers should manage 80 per cent of it. The glen is steep-sided all the way to Loch Etive, and most of it is a continuous descent. At Glen Kinglass Lodge the path turns into a wide dirt road, and progress will be rapid thereafter.

Some care is necessary as the surface is quite loose and you can go very fast, particularly on the downhills. We didn't meet any motor vehicles at all during our journey, but estate Land Rovers could easily be encountered. The nearest public road is still many miles away, and access for motor vehicles is in any case restricted by a series of locked gates.

About halfway down the glen the north bank of the river becomes wooded, mostly with naturally seeded Scots pine. A few bridges lead across the river, but there is no road or path on the other side. Finally you meet Loch Etive and are at sea level. Turn left to cross the River Kinglass on a bridge for vehicles and continue south.

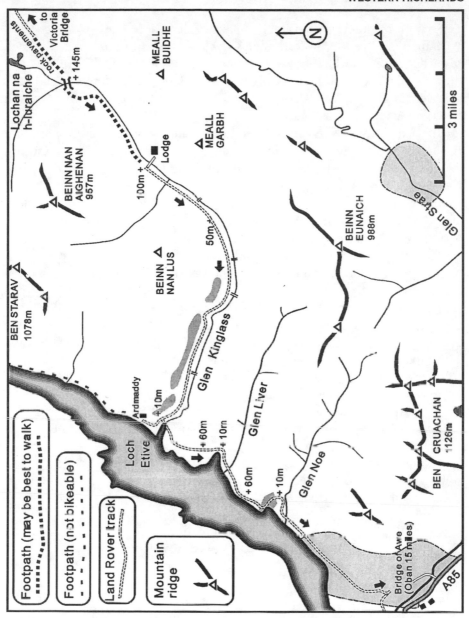

Legend:
- Footpath (may be best to walk)
- Footpath (not bikeable)
- Land Rover track
- Mountain ridge

Map labels: to Victoria Bridge, rock pavements, + 145m, Lochan na h-braiche, MEALL BUIDHE, MEALL GARBH, Lodge, 100m +, BEINN NAN AIGHENAN 957m, 50m +, BEINN NAN LUS, BEN STARAV 1078m, BEINN EUNAICH 988m, Glen Srae, Ardmaddy, + 10m, Glen Kinglass, + 60m, + 10m, Glen Liver, Loch Etive, + 60m, + 10m, Glen Noe, BEN CRUACHAN 1126m, Bridge of Awe (Oban 15 miles), A85, 3 miles, N

Loch Etive (Ardmaddy) to Bridge of Awe

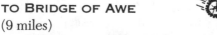

(9 miles)

Your time at sea level will be quite brief. The dirt road south climbs steeply for half a mile, then plunges down to sea level again at Inverliver Bay. Indeed, the whole route from here to Bridge of Awe hardly has a yard of flat.

Your efforts, however, are amply repaid by some absolutely stunning views. Initially these are to the north along Loch Etive, and then across the loch towards the Benderloch hills. Finally, on a long descent to Glen Noe, the massive slopes of Ben Cruachan come into view. This is one of Scotland's grandest mountains, most commonly seen on the other side from the A85 between Tyndrum and Oban.

Cross the River Noe on another bridge and continue south-west into coniferous forest. The road climbs away from the shore for a mile, then swings round to the south-east, descending steadily towards the A85, running through the Pass of Brander.

At the start of the descent there is a T-junction where you should turn left. Before you get to the A85 there are a number of right turns leading to places further west, but there is no bridge over the River Awe west of Bridge of Awe, so this is the only exit point to the public road.

Just before the A85 you pass under the railway line leading to Oban, then finally reach the main road at Bridge of Awe. Just before the main road you will have passed a tea room (there is a sign saying Inverawe, Trout Fishing, Smokery, Nature Trail, Tea Room, open daily). Alternatively, there is a camp site and tea room 400 metres further east on the A85.

It is possible to make this route into a circular one by cycling on public roads to Bridge of Orchy. The way to do this is to travel east on the A85, then turn left on to the B8074, passing through Glen Orchy. The Glen Orchy road is very pretty and fairly quiet; for a mountain-bike route alternative see Glen Orchy. The A85 will be busy in summer. The distance from Bridge of Awe to Bridge of Orchy is 23 miles.

Another alternative is to use the train. The nearest station is Taynuilt, two miles further east. Unfortunately, at the time of writing space on trains for bikes was quite limited, and advance booking is advised. Trains are not frequent.

TYNDRUM TO BRIDGE OF ORCHY

Parts of the West Highland Way and Auch Gleann.

GENERAL NOTES

While the southern part of the West Highland Way is not bikeable, most of the route north of Tyndrum can be cycled over. There are short sections which should not be biked, and alternatives are given.

The West Highland Way is probably the most scenic long-distance route in Scotland. Much of the route follows Caulfield's military road. Major William Caulfield was appointed inspector of roads by General Wade, and carried on General Wade's work for 35 years, building in total 750 miles of roads.

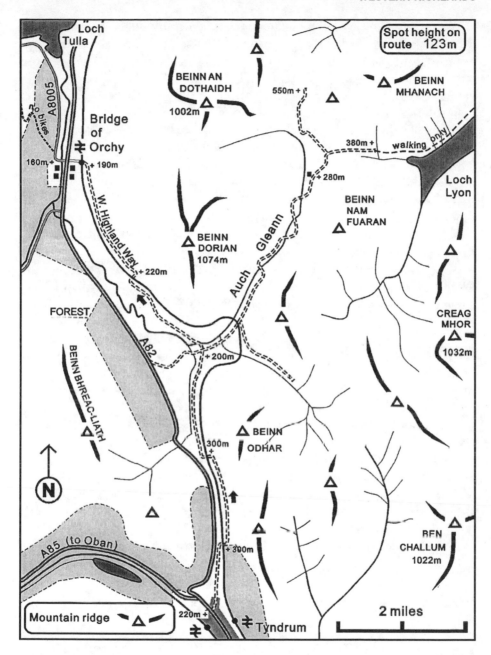

Spot height on route 123m

Loch Tulla

A8005

bikes

BEINN AN DOTHAIDH
1002m

550m +

BEINN MHANACH

Bridge of Orchy

walking only

160m +

+ 190m

380m +

+ 280m

Loch Lyon

W. Highland Way

BEINN NAM FUARAN

Auch Gleann

BEINN DORIAN
1074m

+ 220m

FOREST

A82

CREAG MHOR

1032m

+ 200m

BEINN BHREAC-LIATH

BEINN ODHAR

300m +

N

300m +

A85 (to Oban)

BEN CHALLUM
1022m

Mountain ridge

220m +

Tyndrum

2 miles

Walkers will be encountered all along the West Highland Way. Mountain-bikers should be considerate and give way where necessary.

On no account should cyclists attempt to use any part of the West Highland Way south of Tyndrum. Most of it, in any case, is not passable on a bike.

Tyndrum has good facilities, including a camp site and lots of tea rooms and shops catering for coach parties passing through.

TYNDRUM TO
AUCH GLEANN

This section has a good surface. Start from the West Highland Way signpost near the Green Welly Shop. The route winds up the hill following the old public road to Glen Coe, between the A82 and the West Highland Railway line. The path climbs steeply until it gains the level of the rail line. After this it crosses under the railway, running alongside it for just under a mile, before crossing to the west again to descend into Auch Gleann.

The railway crosses Auch Gleann at high level on the famous twin-viaduct horseshoe curve. This was opened in 1894 and carries the line from the shoulder of Ben Odhar to volcano-like Ben Dorian. The West Highland Way crosses the Ault Kinglass river at a lower level; cross the river to continue north to Bridge of Orchy, or turn right before it to explore Auch Gleann (see next section).

AUCH GLEANN TO
LOCH LYON

An interesting diversion from the West Highland Way between Tyndrum and Bridge of Orchy is to ride up Auch Gleann to Loch Lyon. This is basically a steady climb; occasionally the track is quite rough, but virtually all of it can be ridden.

Coming from Tyndrum, turn right before crossing the river and pass under the northern railway viaduct; after this continue up the track by the river. The track is fairly stony at times and there are several river crossings, some of which are bikeable. The track ends half a mile short of the loch, but the loch is clearly visible.

There is some evidence of an old drove road by the north shore of Loch Lyon but this is not bikeable; connecting up to the public roads in Glen Lyon will require you to push your bike for about seven miles through mixed grass, heather and boggy reeds. The descent back the way you came is fast with some great views.

AUCH GLEANN TO
BRIDGE OF ORCHY

The path crosses the Allt Kinglass river, then heads north-west towards Bridge of Orchy, climbing gently for most of the way. Much of the surface is the original stony path of the old public road. There are good views towards Loch Tulla and the Black Mount hills. Much of the path consists of rounded cobbles compacted through years of use and now grassed over. It could be cycled on any wide-tyred bike.

At Bridge of Orchy station it is necessary to dismount briefly at steps to pass under the railway. After this there is a steep descent to Bridge of Orchy on a public road. There is a hotel and bunkhouse at Bridge of Orchy (but no shop).

The walking route continues north from Bridge of Orchy to Inveroran on a footpath which crosses the hill of Mam Carraigh. Mountain-bikers should not go this way; the A8005 is a good alternative. This is a single-track road and quite quiet. There is a hotel at Inveroran which provides good bar food, and wild camping is allowed just beyond the hotel; there are, however, no toilet facilities for campers.

GLEN ORCHY

A long route south of Bridge of Orchy.

GLEN ORCHY
(8 miles one way)

This is a challenging route, as there are many streams to cross and a steep hill at the southern end. Start at either end; the narrow road with passing places in Glen Orchy is a good way to make it into a circular route. What traffic there is will be slow-moving, and there is beautiful scenery.

There are some great swimming pools in the river at the southern end of the route, and a fine series of waterfalls. The only eating place is the Bridge of Orchy Hotel; this also has a bunkhouse.

From the Bridge of Orchy end cross the bridge beside the hotel, then turn left to a forest road. This lasts for just over a mile, then becomes a rough track.

From the southern end cross the Bailey bridge at Eas Urchaidh and climb steeply up the hill. You bike over several concrete fords on the way up, then come to a flat area where the track ends. Turn right here to cross the river. There is a small forest reserve on the left which you could visit.

After this the route becomes much rougher, although most of the climbing is done. There are lots of burns to cross and another river to wade over at Allt Coire Bhiocair. I guess the direction in which you do the route depends on whether you want to end with a meal or a swim!

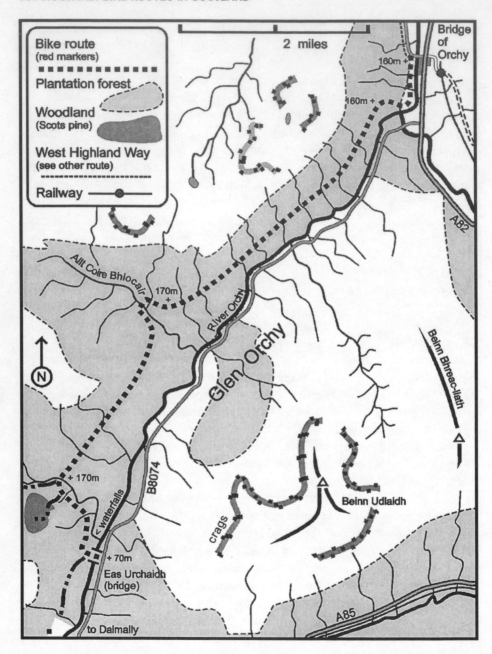

Bike route
(red markers)

Plantation forest

Woodland
(Scots pine)

West Highland Way
(see other route)

Railway

2 miles

Bridge of Orchy

160m +

160m +

A82

Allt Coire Bhiocair

170m +

River Orchy

Glen Orchy

Beinn Bhreac-liath

N

+ 170m

B8074

waterfalls

crags

Beinn Udlaidh

+ 70m

Eas Urchaidh
(bridge)

to Dalmally

A85

GLENACHULISH

Very steep routes near Ballachulish, and one short, easy one.

GLENACHULISH CIRCULAR ROUTE

(4 miles, blue markers)
This begins from a car park half a mile west of the Ballachulish Bridge. Take the minor road leading to South Ballachulish village.

The climb begins gently from sea level, with the river close by. As you climb higher it gets steeper, with the mountain Beinn a Bheithir towering over the forest.

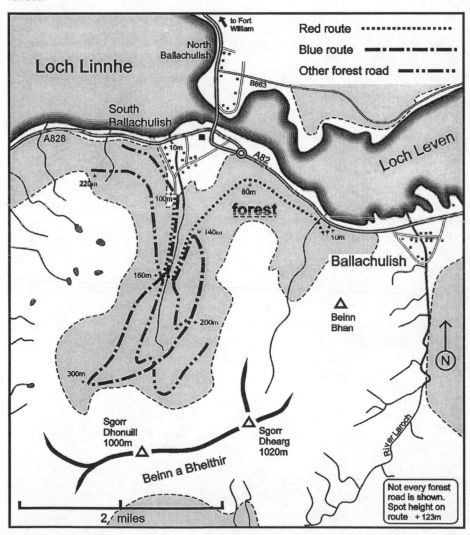

After a mile, at 150 metres, the easier red route forks off to the left; the blue route continues uphill. Much of the forest is of recent planting, so the views are quite open.

As you climb higher up Gleann a Chaolais you get views over Loch Leven and Loch Linnhe; eventually Ben Nevis comes into sight. You reach the summit of the route at about 300 metres.

The descent is gentle at first but after the first crossroads it becomes steeper. You continue to drop steeply until you meet the red route again at 140 metres.

St John's Route
(2 miles, red markers)

This begins at the church and war memorial halfway between Ballachulish and Ballachulish Bridge. There is a short climb, then a flat section taking you round into the glen.

The views up Loch Leven are great, but it's a pity it's not a bit longer. Still, it's a handy way to get to Ballachulish, which has shops, a pub, tourist information and toilets. The Ballachulish Hotel beside the bridge can provide bar meals all day.

LOCH ALINE TO LOCH ARIENAS

Varied bike routes in a scenic area – one long descent.

General Notes
For some reason I had never biked in the Lochaline area. However, a sudden change of plan after cycling in Mull caused me to have an opportunity to go there.

I was surprised at just how lovely it was, with a fair amount of natural forest and torrents of waterfalls everywhere (it was fairly wet at the time!).

This area, being relatively unpopulated, is particularly good for seeing wildlife. Golden eagles are not uncommon, and are unmistakable because of their size; pine martens are on the increase. These look like a stoat or a ferret but are the size of a small cat.

Head of Loch Aline to Savary
(15 miles circular)

The above distance includes six miles by road to complete the circle. Starting from Lochaline (the village, that is), bike north on the A884 for two miles (you aren't likely to be bothered by a lot of road traffic).

Look out for a small gate on your left and follow the blue and red mountain-

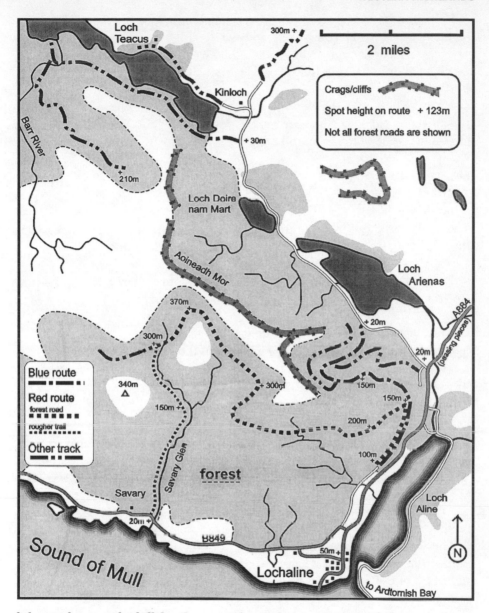

Loch
Teacus

300m +

2 miles

Kinloch

Crags/cliffs

Spot height on route   + 123m

Not all forest roads are shown

+ 30m

Barr River

+
210m

Loch Doire
nam Mart

Loch
Arienas

Aoineadh Mor

370m

+ 20m

20m
+

300m +

+ 300m

150m

150m

A884

(passing places)

Blue route

Red route
forest road

rougher trail

Other track

340m
Δ

150m +

200m

100m
+

Savary Glen

forest

Savary

20m +

Loch
Aline

Sound of Mull

B849

50m +

Lochaline

to Ardtornish Bay

N

bike markers up the hill for about a mile. At the next gate turn left on to a forest road. This is where the blue and red routes diverge.

There are then another three miles of steady climb to do. It's worth it, though, for as you get higher there are great views of Mull and its satellite islands. Look out for a prehistoric cairn at this point.

You reach the summit of the route at 370 metres, passing fairly close to the crags of Aoineadh Mor, then the descent starts.

Very soon after this, when you cross a small burn, look out for a left turn on to an old drove road leading down Savary Glen.

This is a great descent on a mountain-bike; it's also historic, as this is the way cattle were driven from Mull to markets such as Falkirk and Fowlis Wester in Perthshire.

Near the bottom of the glen you pass the ruins of old Savary village, then the remains of an old mill. When you see this you are nearly at the public road. Turn left on to the B849 to return to Lochaline.

HEAD OF LOCH ALINE TO LOCH ARIENAS

(6 miles circular)

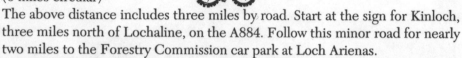

The above distance includes three miles by road. Start at the sign for Kinloch, three miles north of Lochaline, on the A884. Follow this minor road for nearly two miles to the Forestry Commission car park at Loch Arienas.

Follow the blue markers as they climb gently through the forest, keeping straight on at the first junction. There are good views over Loch Doire nam Mart towards Loch Teacus.

After this the route starts going downhill with some sharp bends. It passes a quarry, and after this you meet the junction of the red and blue routes.

Turning right takes you over to Savary on the route previously described; turning left takes you back to the start. Turn left again on to the A884, then left again at the sign for Kinloch.

OTHER OPTIONS

You could explore the other forest roads in the vicinity of the blue route or, more interestingly, continue west until you reach Loch Teacus.

Loch Teacus is an inlet of the larger sea loch Loch Sunart, which separates the Ardnamurchan Peninsula from Morvern.

At Loch Teacus you can either continue round to the north side on a minor road, or you can go round the south side on a forest road.

This eventually curves round to the south-east, following the Barr River for part of the way. You pass a waterfall, then the road and the river separate. A right fork in the forest road leads downstream to a beach; you would have to walk the last bit.

Another option you could try is to go to Ardtornish Bay. This is simply a matter of following the track on the east side of Loch Aline (see map). The bay is just off the map. I believe you pass through some attractive woodland, although I haven't tried this route myself.

LOCAL FACILITIES

There is a hotel in Lochaline, and a small supermarket. I can recommend the hotel's homemade lentil soup (although it was snowing on the May Monday when we called, so perhaps that was what made it taste extra good!). Lochaline is a ferry terminal for Mull, taking you over to Fishnish.

BARCALDINE FOREST

Four forest bike routes in a scenic area; a good option for families.

INTRODUCTION

As with most Forestry Commission bike routes, these are mainly on forest roads. They are fairly varied, but the main attraction of this area is the fine views over Loch Creran and towards Mull and the islands.

There is a disused railway line, but this is so overgrown it is not passable. The railway bridge over the Loch Creran narrows (see map) is passable, however, and a rough track leads up from the road. The main advantage of this is that it cuts out a long section of highway if you are cycling to the north.

Another advantage is that if you are looking for refreshment and don't fancy the Butterchurn Restaurant immediately south of the bridge, you can easily nip across to the Creagan Inn on the other side (where they do good bar lunches).

The Sea-Life Centre nearby is also worth a visit. You can't, however, visit the café without paying an admission charge.

GLEN DUBH
WEE CIRCLE
(5 miles, blue markers)

This begins from the car park at Sutherland's Grove, which is just east of the junction of the A828 and B845.

A small bike path takes you for 100 metres over to the forest entry, then you are off. There may be walkers for the first mile or so.

The route takes you up towards Glen Dubh Reservoir, where you cross a bridge over the outflow. After this you turn right to follow the circle round anti-clockwise.

There is a brief climb, a flatter section, then a longer climb. After this, good views to the west start to appear. The route then turns north again, heading back to the reservoir. Here you turn left again, which takes you back to the bridge once more with a long descent. Return to the start the way you came.

GLEN DUBH
BIG CIRCLE
(8 miles, green markers)

This is slightly more difficult, with a short diversion to the west, then a longer loop to the east. Start as with the Wee Circle, but a mile after the bridge turn right following green markers.

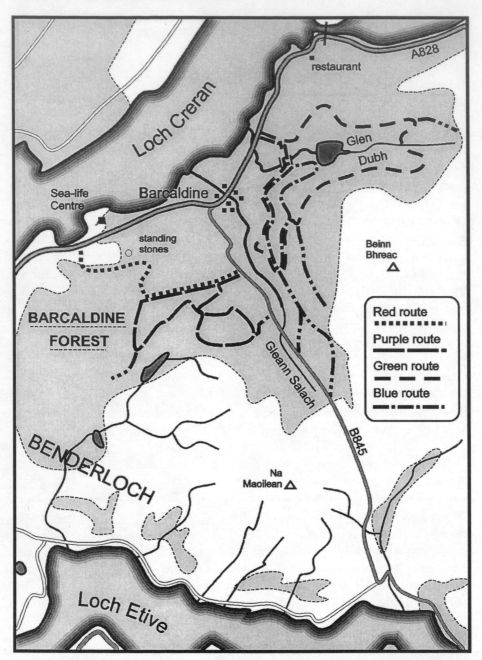

After this the route continues south as before, then turns north again. However, shortly after this, near some Scots pine, instead of descending you bear right on to a forest road that takes you round Glen Dubh at a much higher level.

This climbs again to give great views over Loch Creran, Mull and the nearer island of Lismore. Following this there is a long descent with some flat sections to return to the start.

BARCALDINE FOREST
CIRCULAR ROUTE
(6 miles, purple markers)

This begins a mile up the B845 from the A828 junction. There is a small car park half a mile into the forest.

The route is in fact a figure of eight, and the gradients are fairly gentle, if slightly steeper on the southern loop further up the hill. Again this higher section gives good views of Lismore and Mull.

BARCALDINE FOREST
THROUGH ROUTE
(3 miles, red markers)

This starts the same as the purple route above, unless, of course, you elect to start it half a mile west of the Sea-Life Centre. This is at Mill Farm, which is opposite a small bay.

There are standing stones and a cairn just north of the route near Achaca. Return for this route would have to be on the A828, and this is not recommended for children.

LOCH AVICH AND LOCH AWE

An easy but very scenic route taking in two lochs and a waterfall.

INTRODUCTION
It's often said as a joke that all the Western Isles actually belong to the ferry operator Caledonian MacBrayne. What is certainly true is that Loch Awe side belongs to the Forestry Commission.

For some reason, in this vast swath of land, they've picked out just one mountain-bike route. This is a pity, for there is lots of scope for more than this. However, the route they have chosen is a little gem, with good views of Loch Awe and Loch Avich and lots of interesting scenery in between.

Virtually the entire route is on forest roads; there is only a very short section on public road. What hills there are are relatively easy. The route is signposted with green markers. Reach the route from the minor road from Kilmelford on the A816; from Taynuilt on the A85 (signed Kilchrenan); or from Ford at the south end of Loch Awe.

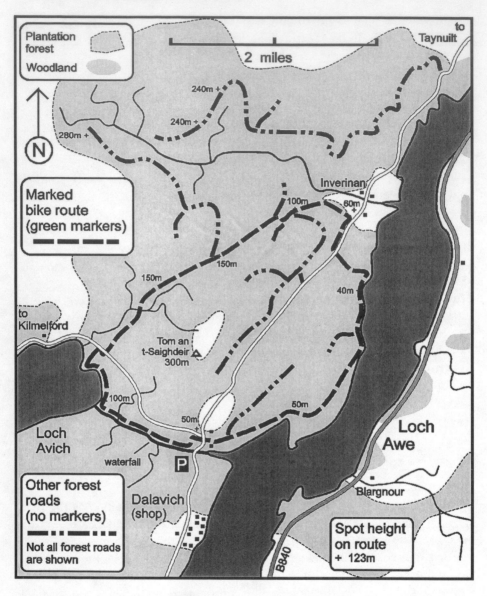

BARNALINE TO INVERINAN

(3 miles)

Begin at the Forestry Commission car park at Barnaline. This is just north of the village of Dalavich. Turn left out of the car park on to the minor road, cross the River Avich, then bear right into the forest at the green mountain-biking sign.

The first half-mile is by the shore of Loch Awe, with Kames Bay continually visible through the trees. This section is flat. Following this there is a gentle climb away from the shore to cross the Barr nam Breacadh peninsula.

There has been some tree-cutting in this area, so there are some open sections. After the peninsula you briefly touch the shore again, then turn right on to the minor road for 500 metres. Near Inverinan you turn left into the forest again at a farmhouse with a small flock of geese.

INVERINAN TO LOCH AVICH
(4 miles)

Climb steadily on this old forest road, which, for a change, is lined with oak trees instead of the usual Sitka spruce.

After a bit you turn right on to another forest road; this has the spruce trees once more, but there are fine open perspectives along it giving good views of the nearby hills.

At the end of this section you meet the minor public road leading to Kilmelford. The forest road is signposted 'Glen Road – no vehicles'. Turn right down the hill here, and after a short distance turn left again into the forest, signposted 'River Road'. There is a short, flat section, then Loch Avich comes into view.

LOCH AVICH TO BARNALINE
(2 miles)

The ride by the shore of Loch Avich is really lovely. At the end of this you meet the River Avich on its short trip to Loch Awe. The river is visible most of the time. Just before the end you meet the Avich Waterfalls. These are really quite spectacular and you can go right up to them. There is a picnic table, so this is a good place for a stop.

Finally there is a further descent and you meet the public road again at the point where you first entered the forest. Turn right here to cross the river and return to the car park.

LOCAL FACILITIES

There are no tea rooms or hotels in the immediate vicinity of the route. There is a small shop and post office in Dalavich. There are two hotels at Kilchrenan, seven miles to the north, both of which can provide food. Eleven miles to the south at Ford, at the southern tip of Loch Awe, there is another hotel that provides bar lunches etc.

When I first biked along the minor road on the west side of Loch Awe it was very quiet. The road is very scenic, but extremely hilly. In recent years the number of holiday homes and chalets has increased considerably, so there is likely to be more holiday traffic in the summer. If you are cycling with children you should bear this in mind.

CARNASSERIE CASTLE ROUTE

Fairly short, fairly difficult and fairly interesting!

INTRODUCTION

While this is another Forestry Commission route, it has a rather different flavour, being mostly on narrow, overgrown tracks rather than forest roads. There are some fallen standing stones in the woods and other archaeological features. There are occasional views of the island of Eilean Righ. The route may be muddy in wet weather; if this is the case you may have to walk some sections.

CARNASSERIE CASTLE
TO LOCH CRAIGNISH
(2 miles)

Begin at the castle car park, which is about a mile north of Kilmartin on the A816 Oban road. There are a number of display boards giving archaeological information.

Bike through the gate and up the dirt road towards the castle. Shortly before the castle turn left out of the woods and follow the purple mountain-bike markers across a field.

This eventually joins another track which leads along the edge of the plantation forest. The track is quite overgrown and there are low branches and a few fallen trees, so some care is necessary.

After a mile the overgrown track joins a forest road, where you turn right (the return loop). There is a gradual descent, becoming steeper, and the forest road curves round to the right, crossing a burn. The island of Eilean Righ comes into view here, together with a small yacht harbour.

Leave the main path here, bearing left on to a grassy footpath that looks as if it's going nowhere. If you see a modern bungalow on your left, you've missed the turning.

LOCH CRAIGNISH
FORESHORE PATH
(2 miles)

At the start of this you are quite near the sea, although it's often obscured by the dense trees. It's definitely got a 'lost in the woods' feel to it, as the surface is mossy and trees overhang, cutting out most of the sky.

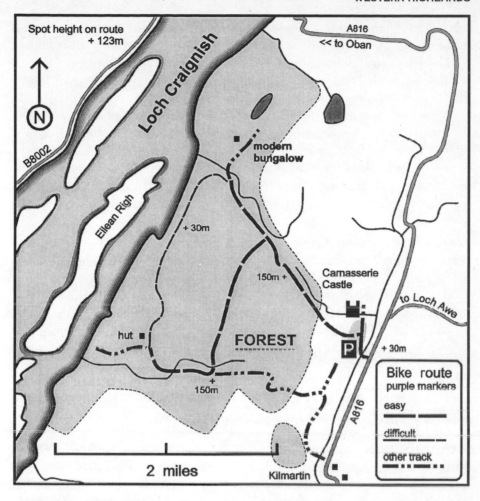

I had no problem biking the path, even though there had been recent rain and the going was quite soft. Both I and my bike needed a good hose down afterwards, though!

You cross a number of tiny streams and the path gradually winds away from the shore. At times it seems as if the route is going to disappear entirely, but it never does.

Eventually you come to a short section that you definitely can't bike. This is a short footpath leading up to a forest road.

RETURN TO CARNASSERIE CASTLE
(5 miles)

When you emerge on to the forest road you see a small building with a wind vane. This stands beside a larger ruin. Turn left here and climb steeply away from the sea shore.

The forest road is quite unexceptional. The trees were all mature when I visited, and while I was passing through they were busy cutting them down, so there may not be any by the time you get there.

After a mile there is a left turn, indicated by a purple mountain-bike marker. Follow this forest road for another two miles. When you get to the next marked junction it should look familiar. Turn right to retrace your way back to the castle.

It's also possible to leave the forest by an alternative route (see map). This is a rapid descent on a wide forest road ending at a quarry near the village of Kilmartin (where there is a shop and hotel). Kilmartin is famous for the sculptured stones in the churchyard.

CARNASSERIE CASTLE

This is open at all reasonable times, and there is no charge for admission. It is looked after by the Scottish Office (Historic Scotland).

It was the home of John Carswell, the first Protestant Bishop of the Isles, who produced the first book ever printed in the Gaelic language. This was John Knox's *Liturgy*, which he translated and published in 1567. The castle itself was blown up in 1685 during Argyll's rebellion.

LOCH GLASHAN AND KILMORY

Two forest routes near Lochgilphead, both with good views.

INTRODUCTION

Both of these routes are entirely on forest roads which are mostly well compacted and fairly smooth; there is always a climb to enter the forest, but after that the gradients are reasonably gentle, making the routes a good choice for parties with children.

LOCH GLASHAN ROUTE

This consists of a circuit round Loch Glashan which is signposted with red markers. The approach from the west is from Kilmichael Glen, and this is fairly gentle. There are also two steeper approaches from the A83 further east.

KILMICHAEL GLEN APPROACH

(3 miles, red markers)

Take the minor road off the A816 three miles north of Lochgilphead, signposted Kilmichael Glassary. Continue along this for two miles, crossing the River Add twice, then turn right towards the forest by an old sawmill, signposted Barrachuile.

This starts off fairly flat, passing a rag-bag of houses and caravans, then climbs into the forest, the River Add tumbling by on the right.

Near the top of the hill you go under a big water pipe. Soon after, turn right at a T-junction. This leads across the river, passing a conservation area with several ponds. After this the marker posts change colour and you are on the Loch Glashan circuit.

The Horseshoe Inn at Bridgend provides bar food; rather more upmarket is the Cairnbaan Hotel two miles further south, which has a view of the Crinan Canal.

LOCH GLASHAN CIRCUIT
(8 miles, red markers)
Obviously this can be done in either direction, although I believe that the views will be best if it is done anti-clockwise.

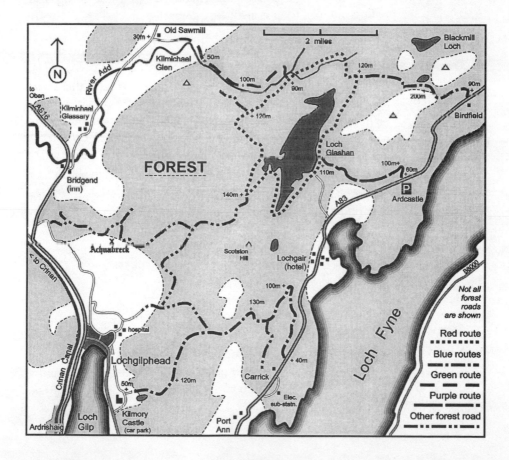

On the east side the route runs close to the loch shore. Great swathes of the forest have been cut down recently, making the foreground look a bit untidy. It does mean, however, that the loch is continually visible.

The route dips down below the dam and there is a bit of a climb to regain the shore level. After this it continues round the southern tip of the loch, turns north again, then begins a steady climb away from the shore to its highest point at 160 metres. After this there is a long descent with fine open views to the conservation ponds.

ARDCASTLE AND BIRDFIELD APPROACHES
(both 2 miles, purple and blue markers)
Both of these approaches begin with a steep climb from the A83 by Loch Fyne.

The Ardcastle approach is two miles north of Lochgair. The car park is in Ardcastle Wood, which is on the east side of the main road. Entry to the bike route (purple markers) is 300 metres further north on the other side of the road. There is a steep climb initially, then it levels off, meeting the red circuit at the Loch Glashan dam.

There is a hotel in Lochgair which can provide bar meals, teas, etc.

The Birdfield approach (blue markers) is at the top of a hill by a white bungalow. Electricity pylons which are clearly visible cross the road at that point. The climb is longer and steeper than the Ardcastle one but there is a fast descent after this to the blue/red junction at the north end of Loch Glashan.

KILMORY TO CARRICK
(6 miles, blue markers)
This begins immediately behind Kilmory Castle where the council offices are located. From the A83 this is signposted Kilmory and Industrial Estate. Continue up through the industrial estate. If you are arriving by car, leave it in the nature trail car park.

Walk your bike towards the castle reception desk, turn right just before the main door and follow a flagstone footpath round the right-hand side of the castle. The bike trail begins at the rear of the staff car park.

This route is not circular so you will have to return the way you came or bike back on the A83. The A83 will be quite busy, so returning the way you came is the better option. There are good views over Loch Fyne from some parts of the route and the mountains of Arran can be seen in the far distance.

If you are joining the route from the east end at Carrick, note that the entry point is one mile north of Port Ann. When you start to see electricity pylons on the east side of the road, you are very near.

ARDNOE AND LOCH SWEEN

Varied bike routes in an area of outstanding natural beauty.

ARDNOE ROUTE
(13 miles)

This route consists of a nine-mile off-road section which takes you north-west towards Ardnoe Point; after this it turns south towards Tayvallich. Return to the start is four miles on the B8025, which is reasonably quiet. The whole route is very scenic, with fine views towards Jura in the middle section. The route is quite hilly; the largest part of it is on forest roads.

Start at the Druim-an-Duin car park, which is on the B8025 between Tayvallich and Crinan. The car park is near a wide bend in the road at the top of a hill (the start point of the Faery Isles route is across the road).

As indicated on the map, the route begins with a steady climb; there is a fine view of the loch Caol Scotnish at a sharp bend. After this there is a further climb through the forest. After about two miles you emerge high above the village of Crinan, with a stunning view over Loch Crinan and the Moine Mhor.

Following this there is a fast descent travelling east; as you turn the corner, the island of Jura comes into view. This north part of Jura is mostly uninhabited, although there are large numbers of deer (the name Jura means 'deer island').

As you work south, the mountains the Paps of Jura slowly become visible. There is a lovely section by the rocky inlet of Sailean Mor; after this there is a gentle climb through forest after you leave the forest road to follow a narrower track.

Finally you leave the trees at a sign for Knapdale Forest. There are some ups and downs, with occasional views of Jura, and eventually you meet the public road by the small pier at Carsaig. Turn left (east) and cycle to Tayvallich.

There is an excellent restaurant and a camp site in Tayvallich. The public road back to the start at Druim-an-Duin is mostly flat, although there is a steep little hill at the end; this section too is very pretty.

FAERY ISLES ROUTE
(6 miles, return distance)

This is a fairly gentle route which could be cycled on any bike. It is mostly in woodland, but also has interesting sea views. You have to return the way you came.

Initially the route is a gentle descent on a dirt road leading through plantation forest. It soon becomes more interesting, however, as the uniform spruce gives way to more varied woodland owned by the Scottish Woodland Trust.

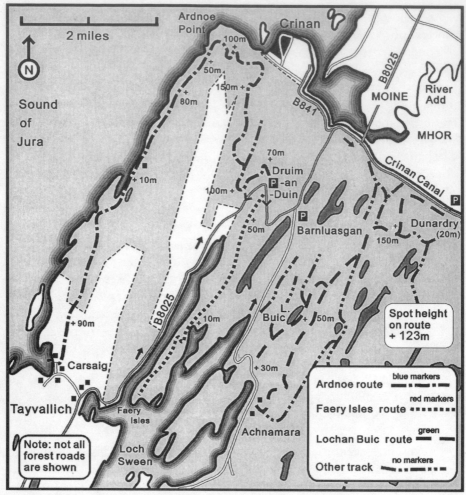

The route passes a number of rocky tidal pools, finally finishing near the tip of the peninsula with a fine view over Loch Sween. This is a great route for young children.

LOCHAN BUIC ROUTE
(9 or 11 miles circular)

This route begins at the Forestry Commission car park at Dunardry on the B841.

At first there is a stiff climb, with a fine view over Kilmartin Glen. After this the route continues to be undulating, with good views from the higher sections.

This area is a mass of forest roads and if you leave the signposted trail, finding your way is likely to be difficult with any map; allow plenty of time if you do leave the way-marked bike route.

As indicated, the signposted route has a longer and a shorter option. The shorter option takes a right turn at Craiglin Loch half a mile before Lochan Buic.

The longer trail misses out Lochan Buic, continuing south to join a minor road at Achnamara; turn right here.

In both cases the return journey is on tarmac; this means that about half the route is on public roads. The minor road and the B8025 are likely to be reasonably quiet; the B841 may be busier. It is possible to cycle along the Crinan Canal towpath; this could be a useful way of getting to the routes at Loch Glashan.

NORTHERN HIGHLANDS

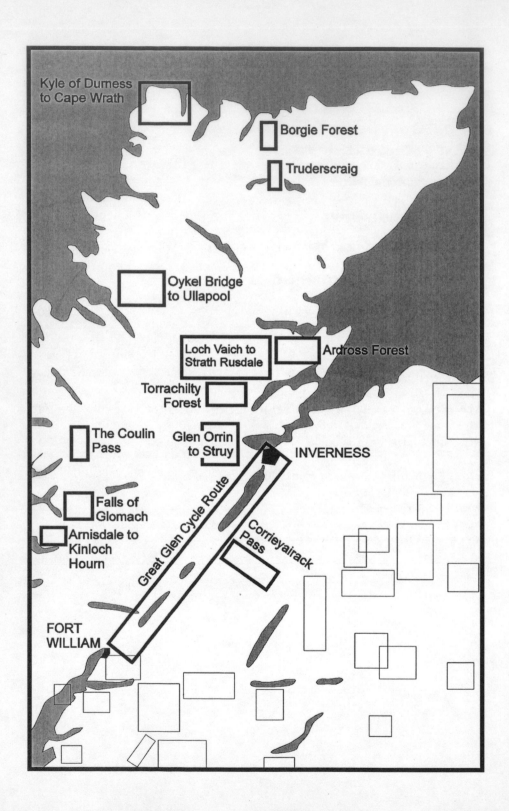

OVERVIEW

Basically, the routes here are all north of the Caledonian Canal; this, of course, links the North Sea to the Atlantic by way of the chain of lochs in the Great Glen. The only exception to this is the Corrieyairack Pass route. This is south of the Caledonian Canal, but it's easily joined up to the Great Glen Cycle Route. It isn't really near any route in Speyside. Because of this I've broken my own rule and put it in the Northern Highlands chapter.

The Great Glen Cycle Route is the longest signposted mountain-bike route in Scotland. At the north end you can make it longer by adding on the Glen Orrin to Struy route. To do this you need to ride a short section on the A833. If even this isn't enough, just tack on Torrachilty Forest, then Loch Vaich to Strath Rusdale. You can even add on Ardross Forest to finally finish at Tain, which is a lovely little town.

It's also possible to extend the Great Glen Cycle Route in a southerly direction, using the northern parts of the West Highland Way. You are only allowed to bike the West Highland Way as far south as Tyndrum; after that it's strictly walking only. This is covered in the Western Highlands chapter.

The remainder of the routes here have to stand on their own but they're very varied, the Arnisdale to Kinloch Hourn route being particularly challenging. The Coulin Pass has no connection with those other mountains, the Cuillins in Skye, apart from the fact that they aren't too far away. It's still got fine views of spectacular mountains, though: Liathach and Beinn Eighe.

The route to the Falls of Glomach doesn't actually go all the way to the waterfall, stopping a mile short, but having a bike is still a big advantage, as it saves a long walk along dirt roads.

As far as routes for young children are concerned, the easier parts of the Great Glen Cycle Route are very suitable, as are Ardross Forest, Borgie Forest and Truderscraig. The last of these also has some archaeological interest.

GREAT GLEN CYCLE ROUTE
Fort William to Laggan

A long route mostly on forest tracks and canal towpaths.

GENERAL NOTES

The Great Glen Cycle Route runs from Fort William to Inverness. Unlike most of the other routes in this book, a few parts of the Great Glen Cycle Route are on public roads. This first section is quite easy, being fairly flat. Much of it is on the Caledonian Canal towpath; naturally, the towpath itself is suitable for children. Later parts of the route, beyond Loch Lochy, are very hilly, with long climbs and steep descents.

The Great Glen forms the dividing line between the Northern Highlands and the Central Highlands. The Great Glen watershed is only 35 metres above sea level. The Cycle Route climbs much higher than this, to over 300 metres at times. You should bear this in mind and be prepared for long, steep climbs. The only alternative route is via the A82, which is narrow and very busy.

FORT WILLIAM TO GAIRLOCHY

(3 miles in Fort William; not for children!)
(6 miles on towpath)

Follow the A82 north out of Fort William, then turn west to the A830, signposted Mallaig. This has a cycle path leading to the canal swingbridge at Banavie.

Turn right here, taking the towpath on the near (east) side of the canal. This passes Neptune's Staircase, the series of eight locks which enables the canal to climb from sea level to 64 feet. There may be pedestrians on the canal towpath, so be considerate.

The Caledonian Canal was designed by Thomas Telford and completed in 1822. The spectacular surrounding scenery is unusual for a canal, particularly the massif of Ben Nevis, the highest hill in Scotland (1,344 metres). The summit is only four miles from the sea and the full sense of its height can be appreciated from the canal. It has the highest sheer cliff face in Britain (1,500 feet), and virtually the only semi-permanent snow patch.

GAIRLOCHY TO CLUNES

(4 miles)

This section is on a public road, the B8005; this is undulating but quite scenic, with good views over Loch Lochy. There is likely to be some light traffic, so it's not suitable for young children.

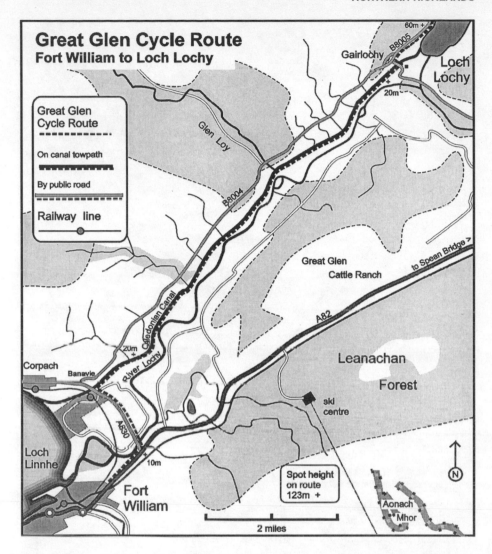

Great Glen Cycle Route
Fort William to Loch Lochy

Great Glen
Cycle Route
- - - - - - - - - - -

On canal towpath

By public road

Railway line

CLUNES TO LAGGAN
(9 miles)

At Clunes turn right by forestry workers' houses into Clunes Forest. Keep beside the loch, as the higher tracks are not continuous. The gradients are mostly gentle. Towards the north end of Loch Lochy the track turns into a road. At Laggan there is a short cycle path leading to Craig Liath Forest by Loch Oich (see next section). Access to Loch Lochy Youth Hostel, which is between Loch Lochy and Loch Oich, is from the A82.

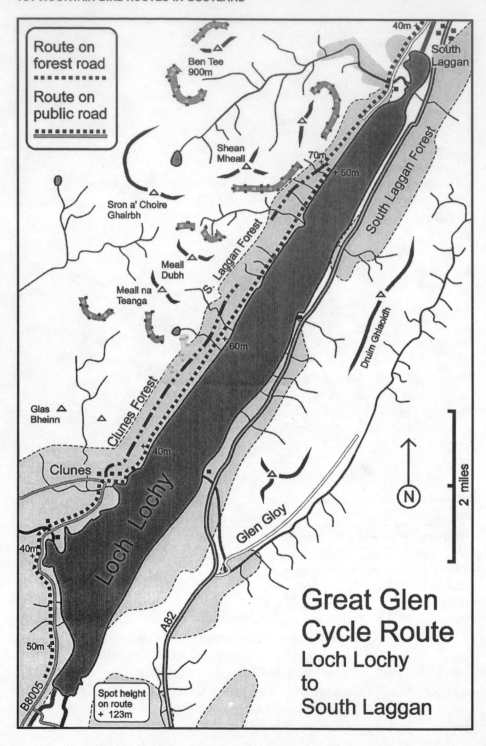

Route on
forest road

Route on
public road

40m
South
Laggan

Ben Tee
900m

South Laggan Forest

Shean
Mheall

70m
+
+ 50m

Sron a' Choire
Ghairbh

S. Laggan Forest

Meall
Dubh

Meall na
Teanga

Druim Ghlaoidh

60m

Clunes Forest

Glas △
Bheinn
△

40m

Clunes

2 miles

Loch Lochy

Glen Gloy

N

40m
+

50m

A82

B8005

Spot height
on route
+ 123m

Great Glen
Cycle Route
Loch Lochy
to
South Laggan

LOCAL INFORMATION

Tourist Information

Fort William: 01397-703781; Fort Augustus: 01320-366367.

SYHA Youth Hostels

Fort William (Glen Nevis): 01397-702336; Loch Lochy (S. Laggan): 01809-501239.

Private Hostels

Ben Nevis Bunkhouse (Glen Nevis): 01397-702240; Fort William Backpackers: 01397-700711; Roy Bridge Grey Corrie Lodge: 01397-712236; Aite Cruinnichidh: 01397-712315.

Bike Shop

Off-beat Bikes, 117 High Street, Fort William; 01397-704008.

GREAT GLEN CYCLE ROUTE

Laggan to Inverness

LAGGAN TO FORT AUGUSTUS
(11 miles)

At Laggan there is a short cycle path leading to Craig Liath Forest by Loch Oich. After a hilly forest section you emerge near Invergarry. The signposted route goes via Mandally, then on to the A82 to cross the River Garry. Turn left on to the A87. Invergarry has a hotel and a tea room (with toilets).

To continue north, join a purpose-built bike path by the public phone box. This climbs steeply, then joins a forest road to descend to Loch Oich.

After this there is another specially built bike path leading to Oich Bridge. After Oich Bridge the route is on the canal towpath; this takes you right into the centre of Fort Augustus. Here the canal descends again, through five locks to enter Loch Ness.

FORT AUGUSTUS TO DRUMNADROCHIT
(22 miles)

From Fort Augustus go north on the A82 for one and a half miles to Allt na Criche picnic site. Turn left into the forest, following green mountain-biking signs.

It's seven miles on hilly forest trails to Invermoriston. There are areas here where the forest has been clear cut – not so attractive, but it does give good views of the loch. There is a long sweep round to the west to make the descent to Invermoriston, then a steep drop to a T-junction where you turn right.

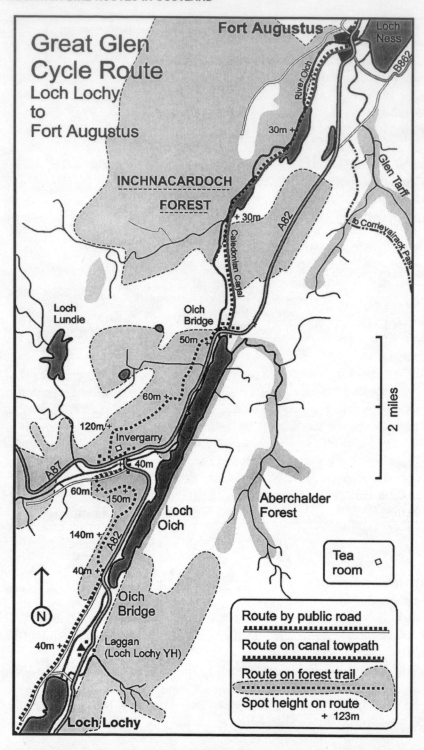

Great Glen Cycle Route
Loch Lochy
to
Fort Augustus

Fort Augustus

Loch Ness

B862

River Oich

30m +

INCHNACARDOCH

FOREST

+ 30m

Glen Tarff

to Corrieyairack Pass

Caledonian Canal

A82

Loch Lundie

Oich Bridge

50m +

60m +

120m +

Invergarry

+ 40m

60m +

150m

140m +

A87

A82

40m +

Loch Oich

Aberchalder Forest

2 miles

40m +

Oich Bridge

N

40m +

Laggan
(Loch Lochy YH)

Loch Lochy

| Tea room | ◻ |

Route by public road

Route on canal towpath

Route on forest trail

Spot height on route
+ 123m

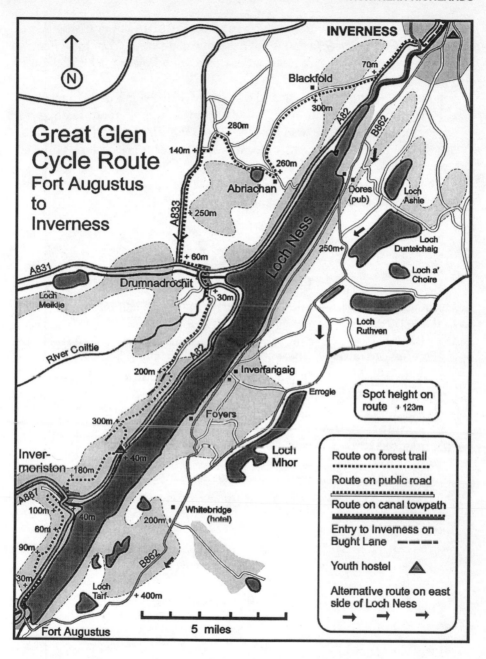

N

**Great Glen
Cycle Route**
Fort Augustus
to
Inverness

INVERNESS

Blackfold

70m +

300m

280m +

A82

B862

140m +

260m

A833

Abriachan

250m +

Dores
(pub)

Loch
Ashie

Loch Ness

250m +

Loch
Duntelchaig

A831

+ 60m

Loch a'
Choire

Drumnadrochit

30m +

Loch
Meiklie

Loch
Ruthven

River Coiltie

A82

200m

Inverfarigaig

Errogie

300m

Foyers

Spot height on
route + 123m

Inver-
moriston

+ 40m

180m

Loch
Mhor

A887

100m +

40m

200m

Whitebridge
(hotel)

60m +

90m +

B862

30m +

Loch
Tarff

+ 400m

Route on forest trail
····························
Route on public road
▪▪▪▪▪▪▪▪▪▪▪▪▪▪▪▪▪▪▪▪▪▪▪▪
Route on canal towpath
▬▬▬▬▬▬▬▬▬▬▬▬▬▬▬
Entry to Inverness on
Bught Lane ─ ─ ─ ─

Youth hostel ▲

Alternative route on east
side of Loch Ness
→   →   →

Fort Augustus

5 miles

At Invermoriston you enter forest again behind the Glenmoriston Arms Hotel. This section is more arduous but has some good views. You climb steeply at first on a surfaced road. After four miles this part ends near Loch Ness Youth Hostel.

The next part is ten miles long and consists of a stiff climb of 300 metres, a high-level section, then a new link to join a minor road leading to Drumnadrochit. The minor road emerges on to the A82 by the River Coiltie. Turn left and bike half a mile to Drumnadrochit. The Loch Ness Monster Exhibition is here.

After Drumnadrochit the route is on roads. It is intended that this section too should be off-road, but there is no date for completion.

DRUMNADROCHIT TO INVERNESS
(24 miles)

At Drumnadrochit turn left on to the A831 for one and a half miles, then right on to the A833 to climb, very steeply, out of Glen Urquhart.

After five miles turn right for Abriachan following the signposted route. In Abriachan turn sharp left for Blackfold, cross moorland and drop to the A82 for Inverness. In Inverness cross the canal bridge, turn east to Bught Lane and follow the river to the town centre.

Hostels
Loch Lochy SYHA: 01809-501239
Fort Augustus (Abbey Backpackers): 01320-366703
Loch Ness SYHA: 01320-351274
Drumnadrochit Backpacker: 01456-450807
Inverness SYHA: 01463-231771

Tourist Information
Fort Augustus: 01320-366367
Inverness: 01463-234353

CORRIEYAIRACK PASS

A high, difficult route joining the Great Glen to Speyside.

GENERAL NOTES

The off-road section of the Corrieyairack Pass runs from just south of Fort Augustus to Melgarve, west of Laggan in Speyside. It climbs from 60 metres at the Fort Augustus end to 770 metres at its highest point.

This military road is one of General Wade's; it was finished in 1731.

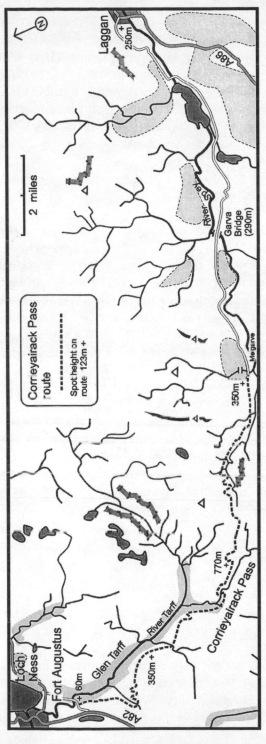

There are three notices at the start at the Fort Augustus end. One tells you that the road over the pass is now an ancient monument and is in the care of the Secretary of State for Scotland (Historic Scotland); it is an offence to damage it. Another notice, by Highland Council, says that motor vehicles are prohibited. The third sign, roughly painted on a gate, says 'walkers only'. This is not so; in fact, there was a charity bike ride recently. The order prohibiting motor vehicles is aimed at four-wheel drives and motorbikes. I have confirmed with Highland Council that mountain-bikes are allowed.

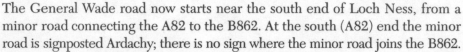

FORT AUGUSTUS APPROACH
(8 miles to summit of path)

The General Wade road now starts near the south end of Loch Ness, from a minor road connecting the A82 to the B862. At the south (A82) end the minor road is signposted Ardachy; there is no sign where the minor road joins the B862.

The first section of the Wade road is badly eroded; there is a metal post to stop vehicles, but I doubt that any vehicle could get up it easily. After that the going gets better. The road climbs south-west at first, to get round the Culachy Burn, passing a fine series of waterfalls. After this it turns south-east and begins the first of the many zigzags it uses to reach the summit of the pass.

The climb is extremely steep, and the surface is quite rocky. Inevitably you will have to walk occasionally. There are brilliant views of the Great Glen and Loch Ness as you climb higher and higher.

Glen Tarff is quite pretty, with remnant pine woods near the river. Eventually you climb completely clear of the glen and the scenery is more forbidding. Finally you reach the summit at 770 metres.

You might think that the worst is over, for all the rest is downhill. Don't be deceived, however; the descent is very steep and rocky, with sharp zigzags in the steepest sections, and extreme care is necessary.

MELGARVE APPROACH
(5 miles to summit of path)
(11 miles Laggan to Melgarve)

You get to Melgarve by taking a minor road from Laggan. This is a pleasant bike ride in itself. As you approach Melgarve the Wade road is clearly visible, climbing steeply up the hill.

One of the Wade bridges is just north of the current bridge here and is worth a short walk to look at. The first section is completely straight; after that the track begins a series of 11 zigzags to get to the top. The fact that the course of these zigzags is still in place indicates just how well the road was surveyed in 1730.

Look back and you can see right over Speyside to the Cairngorms with the River Spey far below. Again the descent on the other side needs extreme care.

While the General Wade road was finished in 1731, the pass was used before this by cattle drovers. Ironically, the first army to use it was the opposition: Bonny Prince Charlie with his Jacobite army.

Once the road was completed, the pass was crossed more regularly. One regular user was the minister of Laggan, who was courting a lady who lived in Fort Augustus. She did eventually consent to become Mrs Grant, so his determination was well rewarded. Probably the most regular users of the road over the pass nowadays are the engineers who service the line of electricity pylons that follow the route. Their vehicles are exempt from the order that prohibits motor vehicles.

It's worth remembering, of course, that at the time the Wade road was built, 'traffic' over it would have been mainly on foot, wheeled vehicles in the Highlands being a rarity. One person said, 'The whole road is rough, dangerous and dreadful, even for a horse. The steep and black mountains and the roaring torrents rendered every step the horse took frightful, and when he attained the summit of the zigzags up Corrieyairack he thought that the horse, man and all would be carried away, so strong was the blast.'

Soldiers occasionally died on the pass from over-fortifying themselves with whisky; make sure it doesn't happen to you!

GLEN ORRIN TO STRUY

A remote track through lonely hills, finishing with a stunning descent.

INTRODUCTION

This is a circular route beginning at the village of Muir of Ord. The first three miles are on a minor road; you then enter a forest, climbing to 260 metres at Orrin Reservoir.

After this the route is less hilly, following a water pipeline for seven miles. There is a steep descent towards Struy with a stunning view.

Return to the start can be via the A831, which is fairly quiet. An alternative is to use the quiet minor road to the south of the River Beauly; this is very attractive.

MUIR OF ORD TO ORRIN RESERVOIR (10 miles)

Start at the train station in Muir of Ord. Turn left out of the station car park on to the A832. After half a mile turn left again by the distillery, signposted Aultgowrie.

After three miles, in Aultgowrie, before crossing the River Orrin, leave the public road by turning left at Loom House Crafts. The access road has a tarmac surface as far as the Orrin Dam.

Keep on the tarmac to remain on the south bank of the river. It is very attractive, with the river close by much of the time, and lots of varied woodland.

After two miles the dam access road is joined on the right by a dirt road crossing the River Orrin. Shortly after this you will meet a locked gate. There is an unlocked side gate for walkers; you may be able to wheel your bike through this by lifting it on to the rear wheel; if not, lift it over.

Shortly after this you leave the forest, passing over a Bailey bridge, and the steep climb to the dam begins; this is made easier by the fact that the surface is still tarmac, rather than loose material. Just before you reach the dam there is a short descent, then a further climb.

ORRIN RESERVOIR TO STRUY
(13 miles)

The route passes over the two dams, the first being a concrete structure which is quite large as Scottish dams go. The second dam is smaller and made of earth; here the route turns into a rough Land Rover track.

After the reservoir the route turns south then east, mostly following the 310-metre contour, as it was originally made to construct the pipeline which you will occasionally see. Despite the pipeline the overall impression is of wild remoteness. This is in fact quite accurate, for not many people come here.

The route briefly dips south to maintain its height as it crosses a burn, then starts to climb more steeply towards the hill of Cnoc Eille Mor (403 metres). There is a sudden panoramic view to the south and east, looking over the Beauly Firth towards the North Sea and Aberdeen, then the descent begins.

At first the descent is fairly gentle, but after you pass reedy Loch Ballach it steepens dramatically, passing crags on the right-hand side. The view is spectacular but it's advisable to stop if you want to look at it.

At the end of the descent there is an interesting little dip crossing a burn, then a fairly flat section leading to Loch Fada. You enter forest here, passing through a gate with a stile for walkers.

Finally, there is more descent through the forest. You finish at Erchless Cottage, which is a short distance from the public road.

Note: if you are doing the route in the opposite direction, enter the forest by turning left on to an older forest track immediately after the cottage. There is no marker but someone has painted three red spots on the gate post. There is no sign at the public road for the cottage but access is at a wide dirt road which climbs steeply. It is immediately east of Erchless Castle.

STRUY TO
MUIR OF ORD

(13 miles by shortest route)

Return to Muir of Ord is by turning left on to the A831. The A831 is usually fairly quiet. The Struy Inn is in the opposite direction but is quite near and serves bar food at lunchtime and in the evening.

Another refreshment alternative halfway between Struy and Beauly is the Wild Bird Centre (see map), which has a tea room. This is only open in the daytime. Beauly has a wide choice of pubs, hotels and carry-out food places.

A more attractive route back to the start is to cycle on the minor road to the south of the River Beauly. This is slightly further (two miles extra), but if you are diverting to go to the pub at Struy you might as well return that way, as it will be virtually the same distance from there.

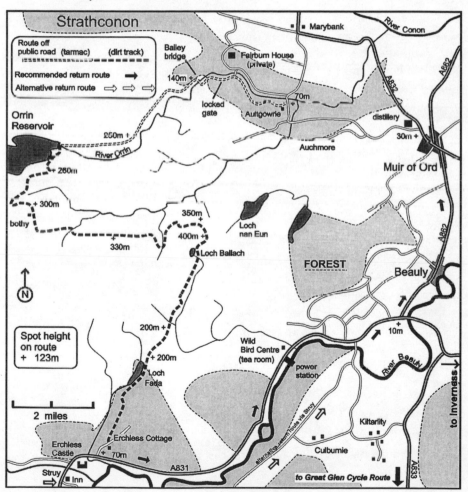

Torrachilty Forest (Strathpeffer)

A varied forest bike route in a scenic area; lots of waterfalls!

General Notes

This route can be done as a circular route starting and finishing in Strathpeffer. Alternatively it makes a good through route maybe beginning at Strathpeffer or Contin and finishing in Garbat Forest.

There are two other bike routes in the vicinity which can be used to extend this one: Loch Vaich to Strath Rusdale to the north, or the Great Glen Cycle Route.

Strathpeffer was a popular spa in Victorian times, and a special train, the Strathpeffer Express, ran regularly from London; you can still sample the waters.

The rainfall here is much less than further west; often while Fort William is dull and grey, this area is enjoying sunshine.

Strathpeffer is a good base for exploring the area; it has a youth hostel and plenty of hotels and B&Bs. The former railway station has been converted into tourist shops. It's got a good tea room, too, which is an excellent place to finish your ride!

Strathpeffer Circular

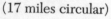

(17 miles circular)

Begin in Strathpeffer and take the A834 north out of the town, heading towards Dingwall. Half a mile after leaving the town, turn left up a minor road for Achterneed.

This is fairly flat at first, then it climbs steeply, passing over the North Highland Railway. Immediately after this there is a sharp right turn; follow this round to the east for just under a mile, then turn left to a road leading into the forest at the Heights of Keppoch.

Quite soon this turns into a forest road, but the climbing doesn't stop; eventually, after half a mile, it eases off and there is a gradual descent towards the river, the Abhainn Sgitheach.

There are some more ups and downs, but the main climb is done. The route slowly curves round to the west, then begins its long descent south-west to Loch Garve.

You have to turn left just before Loch Garve to do the circular route. You pass under the railway again to travel south-east to Contin. Even if you are doing this it's best to continue slightly beyond this junction to have a proper look at the loch.

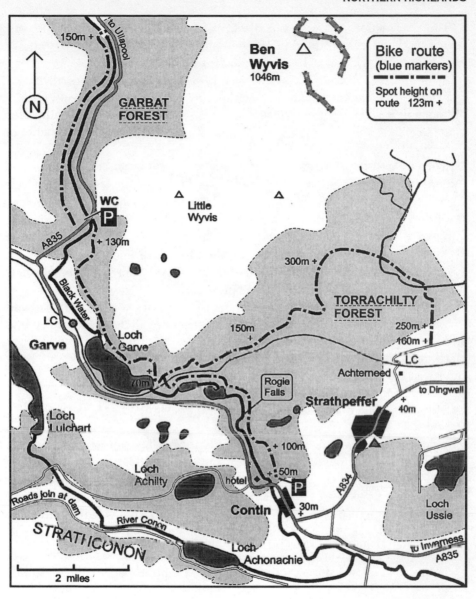

Bike route
(blue markers)

Spot height on
route   123m +

N

150m +
to Ullapool

GARBAT
FOREST

Ben
Wyvis
1046m

WC
P
+ 130m

A835

Black Water

Little
Wyvis

300m +

TORRACHILTY
FOREST

250m +
160m +

LC

Garve

LC

Loch
Garve

150m
+

Achterneed

to Dingwall

+
40m

70m
+

Loch
Lulchart

Rogie
Falls

Strathpeffer

Loch
Achilty

+ 100m

+ 50m

hotel

P

Roads join at dam

Loch
Ussie

Contin

30m
+

River Conon

STRATHCONON

Loch
Achonachie

to Inverness
A835

2 miles

197

The next section, following the Black Water, is very attractive. On the way you pass several lochans, then the Rogie Falls. These are some of the prettiest waterfalls in Scotland; take time off to look at them.

After the falls the route leaves the river, keeping at a high level; finally there is a steep little descent to Contin. Strathpeffer is just a couple of miles away, although up a hill!

GARBAT FOREST ROUTE
(12 miles, Contin to Garbat)

As mentioned earlier, this makes a good linking route to join up to Loch Vaich. It's worth doing on its own, though, and it's less hilly than the Strathpeffer Circular. It's also very pretty around Loch Garve.

Assuming you are beginning at Contin, the route begins at a Forestry Commission car park half a mile north of the A835/A834 junction. There is also a walk directly beside the river; this is not intended for bikes.

There is a bit of a climb to start with, but after that it's fairly easy all the way to Loch Garve. The route doesn't follow the loch shore all the way round, but it still gives excellent views.

It's possible to leave the route and enter the village of Garve using a little track that crosses the river near a graveyard. You can get tea and coffee etc. in Garve and there is a small shop.

After Garve the route uses the bridge on the main road, the A835, to cross the river. There is a car park immediately next to the bridge on the other side. This has toilets and an excellent view of the waterfall, but the actual bike route is just beyond it, signposted as usual with a blue marker.

The route on the west side of the Black Water is fairly flat with wide, open views towards Ben Wyvis. Finally it ends at a bridge just north of Garbat, where it meets the main road. The A835, the main road to Ullapool, is reasonably wide and OK to cycle on, but it isn't suitable for young children.

LOCAL INFORMATION
Strathpeffer Tourist Information: 01997-421415; Strathpeffer Youth Hostel: 01997-421532. The minor road up Strathconon is well worth exploring.

Loch Vaich to Strath Rusdale

A remote mountain-bike route in the Northern Highlands.

Introduction

This route presents no real difficulty, being entirely on Land Rover track. It is very scenic but long and remote; a tool kit is essential, as are warm, waterproof clothing and sufficient food.

While it is inadvisable to bike the route entirely alone (two or three is the ideal number), organisers of larger groups should restrict themselves to signposted mountain-bike routes such as the Great Glen Cycle Route. Do not use this route during the stalking season (Aug–Oct) without checking locally first.

Black Bridge to Deanich Lodge

(10 miles)

Begin at Black Bridge, which is eight miles north of Garve on the A835, between Inverness and Ullapool. Black Bridge is a modern concrete structure. There is a small wooden hut near the bridge, and an open area where cars can be parked.

Begin on the access road for Loch Vaich dam, but after two miles turn right just before a timber bridge and pass through a (locked) metal gate using the side gate for walkers. After this the route is straightforward. Turn right through another gate just before Deanich Lodge.

Deanich Lodge to Lochan a Chairn
(15 miles)

This whole section is very attractive, with Scots pine woodland. When passing Glencalvie Lodge, follow the footpath signs. Dismount and walk in the area of the house if appropriate.

After Glencalvie Lodge there is a gentle climb up Glen Calvie, then a steeper climb when you turn east to Lochan a Chairn.

Lochan a Chairn to B9176
(12 miles)

This begins with a short climb, then is mainly downhill. At two miles you meet boulders on the track to stop cars; after five miles you join a minor road.

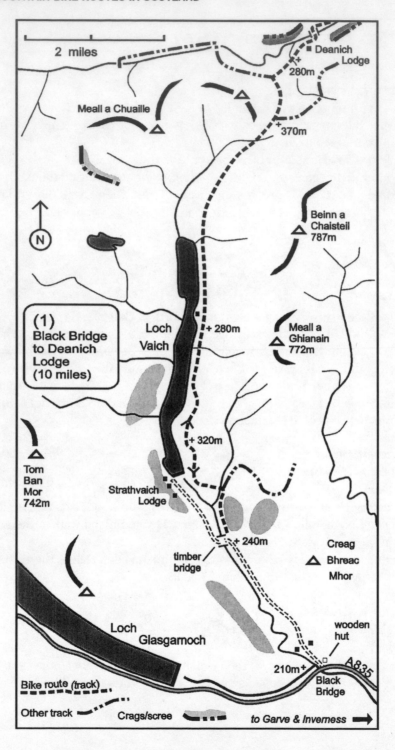

2 miles

N

Deanich Lodge
+ 280m

Meall a Chuaille

+ 370m

Beinn a Chaisteil 787m

(1)
Black Bridge to Deanich Lodge (10 miles)

Loch Vaich

+ 280m

Meall a Ghianain 772m

Tom Ban Mor 742m

+ 320m

Strathvaich Lodge

+ 240m

Creag Bhreac Mhor

timber bridge

wooden hut

Loch Glasgarnoch

210m +

Black Bridge

A835

Bike route (track)

Other track   Crags/scree   to Garve & Inverness →

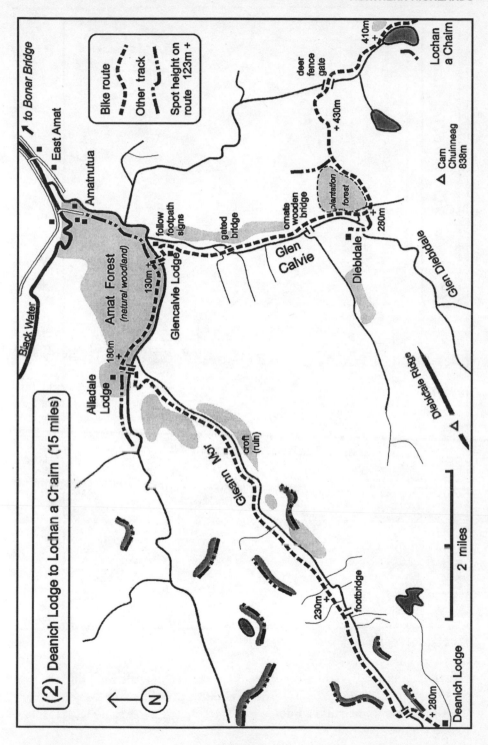

(2) Deanich Lodge to Lochan a Chairm (15 miles)

Bike route

Other track

Spot height on route 123m +

to Bonar Bridge

East Amat

Amatnutua

Black Water

Amat Forest
(natural woodland)

Alladale Lodge

130m +

130m +

follow footpath signs

Glencalvie Lodge

gated bridge

ornate wooden bridge

Glen Calvie

plantation forest

280m +

Diebidale

Glen Diebidale

Diebidale Ridge

deer fence gate

430m +

410m +

Lochan a Chalm

Carn Chuinneag 838m

Gleann Mor

croft (ruin)

230m +

footbridge

2 miles

Deanich Lodge

280m +

N

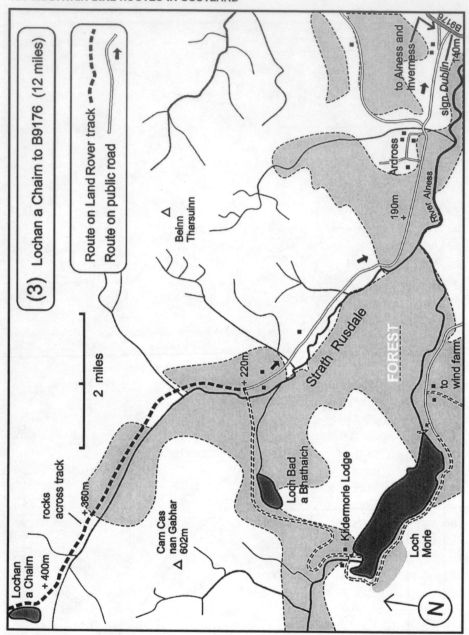

(3) Lochan a Chaim to B9176 (12 miles)

- - - Route on Land Rover track
—— Route on public road

2 miles

Beinn Tharsuinn △

to Alness and Invernesss

B9176

140m

sign Dublin

Ardross

190m +

River Alness

Strath Rusdale

+ 220m

FOREST

to wind farm

rocks across track

Carn Cas nan Gabhar △ 602m

+ 360m

+ 400m

Lochan a Chaim

Loch Bad a Bhathaich

Kildermorie Lodge

Loch Morie

N

RETURN TO START

(extra 32 miles)

Use the minor roads to the west of the A9 as far as Dingwall, then the A834 via Strathpeffer, then the A835. The whole circuit can be done in a day if you are fit. Alternatively you could combine the Torrachilty Forest route with this one to make a two-day tour.

Oykel Bridge to Ullapool

Great scenery; Land Rover tracks and paths; 21 miles.

Introduction

Most of this route is bikeable, but there is a one-mile walking section. There are some fast and challenging downhill runs.

The route passes fairly close to interesting mountains including Beinn Dearg and Seana Bhraigh, giving scenic views. There is a variety of woodland: Scots pine, birch and plantation forest. Check locally during the stalking season (Aug–Oct) before doing this route.

Oykel Bridge to Lochan Badan Glaslaith
(10 miles)

Oykel Bridge is on the A837, 18 miles by road from Bonar Bridge. The only building visible is the Oykel Bridge Hotel. This is mainly used by anglers, but they seemed quite happy to serve food to a couple of mountain-bikers.

Take the minor road opposite the hotel travelling south. This turns into a dirt road opposite a few council houses; shortly after this you meet a bridge over the River Einig. Turn left over the bridge, then bear right to travel south-west.

This starts as a wide forest road, climbing gently. The river is occasionally visible. Bear right at any junctions to keep near the south bank. Four miles after the bridge you emerge from the forest, and shortly after this you meet a small building now used as an animal-feed store. Soon after this you meet a concrete bridge crossing the Corriemulzie River; cross this and turn left.

The climb continues, the river tumbling by on your left and lots of birch trees on the far bank. A forest plantation is just visible on your side. You pass a timber cottage, then Corriemulzie Lodge; this is not the usual imposing highland lodge, being more like an urban bungalow. At this point the high mountains of Beinn Doarg and Seana Bhraigh come into view.

About two miles after the lodge the track divides into two; take the right fork. The left fork continues by the river in to the impressive Coire Mor in the shadow of Seana Bhraigh. This is an interesting diversion but you would have to walk after a while.

Taking the right fork, start to climb out of Strath Mulzic towards Glen Douchary. There is a narrow ravine with the burn of Allt nan Caorach running through it towards Loch an Daimh. The Land Rover track crosses the head of the ravine, heading south to Lochan Badan Glaslaith. You have to leave it and walk a rough footpath leading off to the west 300 metres *before* crossing the burn. You should be on the top lip of the ravine. Do not be tempted down into the steep sides by deer tracks.

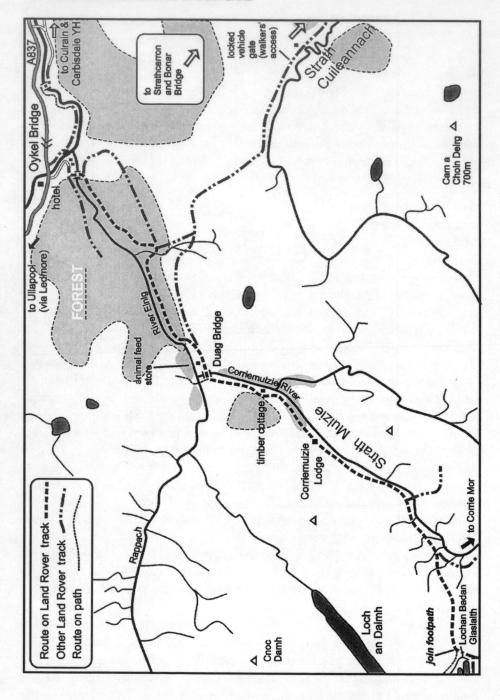

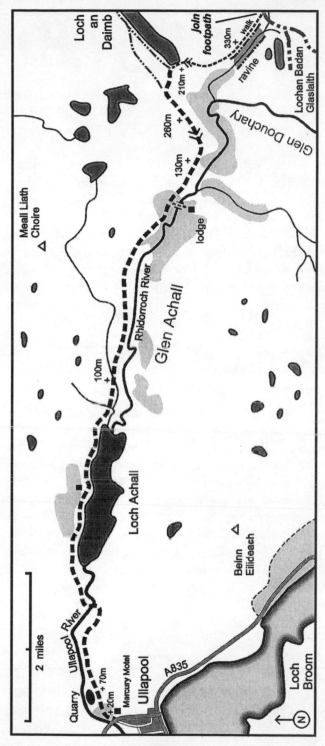

Lochan Badan
Glaslaith
to Ullapool
(11 miles)

The path curves round to the north-west, the side of the ravine opens up, woods at the foot of Glen Douchary come into view and the path starts to be bikeable.

There is a steep descent to the foot of Loch an Daimh; turn left on to a Land Rover track on the far side to continue west.

There is a steady climb away from the loch, a flatter section, then a very steep descent into Glen Achall on a scree surface. After this the difficulties are over.

Pass East Rhidorroch Lodge, surrounded by trees, then a long, flat section leads past Scots pine woods towards Loch Achall.

At Loch Achall you pass Rhidorroch House, then, after the loch, cross the Ullapool River for the final two-mile descent towards Ullapool. Just before the main road you pass a quarry, then there is a steep descent through woods to the main road near the Mercury Motel. To enter Ullapool cross the A835 to a minor road by a filling station.

The Falls of Glomach

Two easy and scenic bike routes, with an optional walk to the waterfall.

Introduction

The Falls of Glomach is easily the most spectacular waterfall in Britain. Surprisingly, many people are quite disappointed when they see it. This is because only a small part of it is visible from the footpath – to see it properly you need to do a bit of scrambling and you need to have a good head for heights.

A mountain-bike is a big advantage if you are going to the waterfall; approaching from the south it reduces the walk in by about 60 per cent. If you are using the northern approach, via Glen Elchaig, you'll be able to bike to within a mile of the waterfall. The northern approach is much more scenic.

Both bike routes are worth doing in themselves, and there are a number of different options you can take to extend your biking route if you prefer not to do any walking. If you are going to the waterfall, good footwear with lugged soles is essential.

Route via
Glen Elchaig
(14 miles, A87 to Iron Lodge)

Start from the road junction just north of Dornie on the A87, signposted Sallachy, Killilan and Camasluinie. If you are getting there by car, a convenient place to leave it is the free church car park just after the junction.

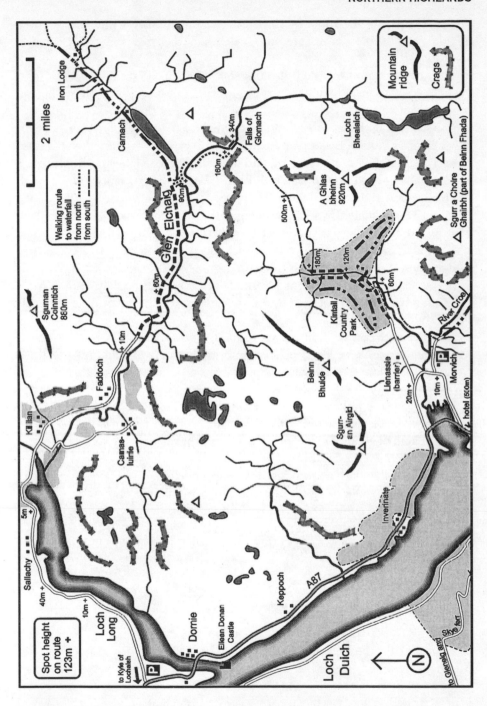

The first part of the route by Loch Long is public road; a mile or two after this the road becomes a private one, with a sign that this is as far as cars are allowed.

The tarmac continues for a little after this, then you are on a dirt road. There are occasional tarmac sections after this, presumably where erosion has been a problem.

The scenery, both by the loch and in the glen itself, is ruggedly beautiful, with steep cliffs and lots of Scots pine further up the glen. Every time I've been up there I've seen deer quite close by, although this is more likely in the winter.

The walking route to the waterfall from Glen Elchaig is marked by a small footbridge over the River Elchaig. There is no sign but it can be identified by a National Trust plaque. If you are walking to the waterfall you might as well lock your bike to the bridge, as you won't be able to take it any further.

If walking isn't your scene you can carry on past Loch na Leitreach to Iron Lodge. Despite its name, this is quite an ordinary building.

It's possible to continue biking beyond Iron Lodge, although it is much more difficult. A very steep track used by four-wheel-drive vehicles leads east towards Loch Mullardoch.

Another path, only slightly less difficult, leads north-east towards Loch Mhoicean. A couple of locals offered an opinion that you could bike to Loch Carron; as we were there in winter the day was too short to check this out – it's a long way.

While you are only a mile from the Falls of Glomach at the Eichaig footbridge, the distance actually walking is just under one and a half miles; there is also a climb of about 250 metres. The last part involves some scrambling; it is not recommended for children.

The waterfall looks quite modest as you approach it, as you only see the very top. To see the whole thing it's necessary to get quite close, then climb some way down into the gorge. Once you've dropped about 20 metres there is a little ledge it's necessary to hang over to get a full view. By now you will be very near, and an 18mm super-wide-angle lens is necessary for a full photo.

ROUTE VIA KINTAIL COUNTRY PARK

(4 miles, NT car park to when walking becomes necessary)

The car park for the Falls of Glomach is at the National Trust visitor centre at Morvich.

The private road past Lienassie Farm has a sign directing cars to the visitor centre car park. There is a barrier at the farm to stop high vehicles, and a locked gate a mile further up.

The effect of all this is to increase the walking distance by about two miles. This is no problem for bikes, though, as you can bike all the way through the forest, which *reduces* the walk in by two and a half miles.

You've still got another two and a half miles to go after this, though, but it isn't a man-made obstacle that prevents you from biking this, just the fact that the twisting path climbs 200 metres over a 400-metre distance!

There are some other places you can go on a bike. The country park isn't signposted for mountain-biking but it isn't so large you'd easily get lost. Crossing over the river gives access to more tracks.

Another option would be to take the road past Morvich and continue along this by the River Croe. This is a Land Rover track for just over four miles. After this it becomes a footpath leading over to Glen Affric. This climbs steeply over the shoulder of Beinn Fhada, so you can't bike over.

THE COULIN PASS

Dramatic mountain views and a fine sense of space.

INTRODUCTION

Despite its similar-sounding name, the Coulin Pass has nothing to do with those other mountains, the Cuillins on Skye. Mind you, it's quite near Skye, being about 20 miles east of Kyleakin, and the mountain views of Beinn Eighe and Liathach are every bit as interesting as the serrated ridges of the Skye Cuillins.

The Coulin Pass runs between the A890 in Glen Carron to the A896 in Glen Torridon. The off-road section is eight miles long, and most of it is Land Rover track. The route can be made circular (see map).

This is not a signposted bike route; you will be biking on other people's property. For this reason any group larger than two or three should ask permission.

THE COULIN PASS
(8 miles)

Start from the A890, at the sign for Achnashellach railway station. This is 13 miles west of Achnasheen, and nine miles east of Lochcarron village. Take the narrow track that leads up to the station.

After a short climb you meet the railway line; cross directly over, obeying the safety precautions on the notice board, and continue uphill. After a short distance you meet a forest road; bear right following the sign 'Coulin Road – no cars, please'.

After this it's simply a matter of keeping straight on up the hill. The climb is

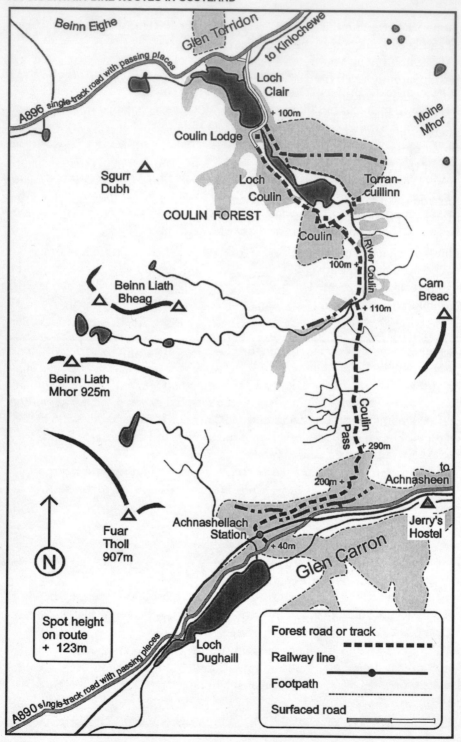

continuous to the summit of the pass at just under 300 metres. Ignore any turn-offs and keep straight on, using the main track.

About halfway up you pass a couple of rather battered American redwood trees, apparently saved from the forester's chainsaw by the word 'leave', painted boldly on their trunks.

There are fine views right across Glen Carron to the hills on the other side, then the trees thin out. You get a distant view of Beinn Eighe as you reach the summit of the pass.

After this the track becomes a bit rougher, but is still easily bikeable. There is a level section, then a long descent over two miles towards the River Coulin.

As you descend, Beinn Eighe gradually becomes clearer and the pinnacles of Liathach, the next mountain on the left, come into view.

The mountain on the immediate left, Beinn Liath Mhor, is interesting too. A hillwalker we met said he had seen a couple of golden eagles the previous day.

When you meet the River Coulin, cross the bridge and turn right to continue in a northward direction. This next section of about a mile is flat. By now the big mountains are in full view, and remnants of Scots pine forest give you an idea of how most of Scotland must have looked hundreds of years ago. You meet

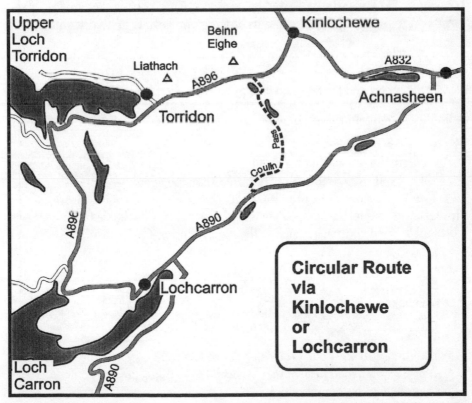

another T-junction beside the big house at Coulin, and here you can go either way.

There are two large houses in the Coulin Estate: Coulin Lodge, which is near Loch Clair, and the house you are presently at. Both are white harled buildings with slate roofs. Coulin Lodge is in trees.

Turning right at Coulin takes you towards the cottage at Torran-cuillinn. This is the preferred way for walkers to go. Beyond the cottage there is a mile of rough footpath; some walking may be required.

The alternative is to turn left and continue on the estate dirt road, passing Coulin Lodge and meeting the footpath again by Loch Clair. The final section by Loch Clair is on a tarmac surface.

RETURN BY PUBLIC ROAD
(25 or 37 miles)

There will be tourist traffic in summer; however, most cars will be slow-moving, as much of the road is single-track with passing places (bikes don't need to wait). The scenery on the long way, via Torridon, is unsurpassed.

There is a food shop and youth hostel in Torridon village, and a hotel serving bar meals just beyond at Annat. Lochcarron village has tea rooms, shops and B&Bs. You can also get refreshments at Kinlochewe and Achnasheen.

ARNISDALE
(LOCH HOURN) TO KINLOCH HOURN

A challenging mountain-bike route in remote country.

GENERAL NOTES

To my mind, the interesting bike routes are the ones that you can barely manage on a bike – and this one certainly falls into that category.

In addition, it's quite difficult to get to; even the roads that lead to it go through wild, remote country. The best plan is just to bike these too. The views, both on the road approaches and on the mountain-bike route itself, are amazing.

ARNISDALE (LOCH HOURN) TO KINLOCH HOURN
(9 miles)

Join the route just south of Arnisdale. There is a right of way from Corran, but you'd have to walk this. Just south of Arnisdale the path towards Kinloch Hourn has a sign saying 'no motor vehicles'.

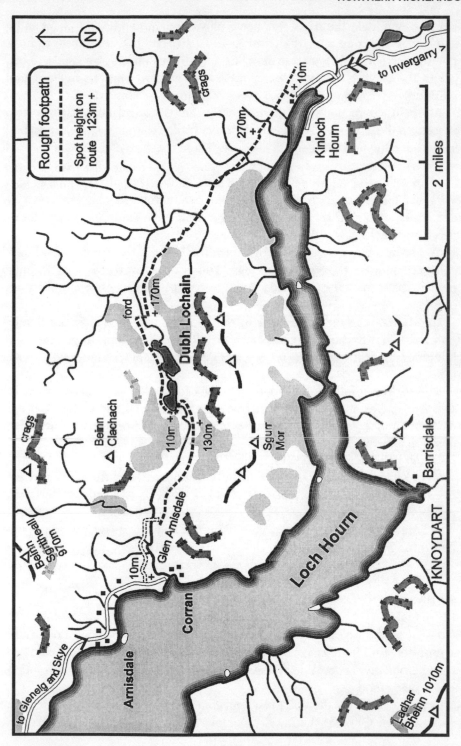

N

Rough footpath

Spot height on route 123m +

to Invergarry >

+ 10m

270m +

Kinloch Hourn

2 miles

ford

+ 170m

Dubh Lochain

crags

Beinn △ Clachach

crags

△

110m +

130m +

△ Sgurr Mor

△

△

△ Barrisdale

Glen Amisdale

△ Beinn Sgritheall 970m

10m +

Corran

Loch Hourn

KNOYDART

Arnisdale

to Glenelg and Skye

Ladhar Bheinn 1010m △

From Arnisdale the track starts smoothly enough, and it's flat as far as the first bridge. After crossing the River Arnisdale it's still bikeable. It then climbs steeply, rising over 100 metres in under half a mile. This is impossible to bike up. In the steeper sections, winter rains have washed away all soft material, meaning you have to push or carry your bike up a boulder surface.

After this there is a short flatter area, which is just bikeable, then a steep descent to the Dubh Lochain lochs. A timber bridge crosses the river and a path leads round the north side of the first loch. There is a short climb past a waterfall to the second loch.

It's possible to bike round the second loch, and you have to if you don't want to get wet feet. This may happen anyway, though, as you probably won't be lucky in all the puddles. At the top of the second loch there's another bridge, then a rough track, which is still mostly bikeable.

You cross a burn, then go up the north bank of the river, meeting a line of pylons running north-west to south-east. The pylons cross the river, and a rough path can be seen on the other side. You have to cross the river to continue south-east.

Cross as soon as possible, as biking on the north bank is impossible. There's no bridge, but if you pick your spot carefully you'll be able to get across by jumping from stone to stone, using your bike to balance. Don't cross if the river is high.

The path now follows the pylons. This is a footpath, not an access road. It's mostly bikeable, although there are several interesting burns to splash through. After two miles there is a view of Loch Hourn far below to the right, then a climb to join a wider track. This has to be walked in places.

When you reach the top you are at 270 metres. There is then a very steep drop to Kinloch Hourn over two-thirds of a mile. Turn right through a gate into trees and don't continue on the pylon track. Pass by the stalkers' cottage to the public road at Loch Hourn.

What's it like? One guy on a Cannondale mountain-bike said it was brilliant – better than anything in Canada.

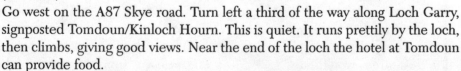

Approach from Invergarry
(27 miles)

Go west on the A87 Skye road. Turn left a third of the way along Loch Garry, signposted Tomdoun/Kinloch Hourn. This is quiet. It runs prettily by the loch, then climbs, giving good views. Near the end of the loch the hotel at Tomdoun can provide food.

After Loch Garry the countryside becomes wilder. There is a climb to the dam at Loch Quoich, then, halfway along Loch Quoich, you pass over the

Quoich bridge, a long finger of the loch pointing northward towards the high Cluanie Ridge. Not long after the bridge, the road starts a 200-metre plunge to sea level.

APPROACH FROM GLENELG
(13 miles from Skye ferry)
Approach Loch Hourn either by catching the Glenelg ferry from Skye (01599-511302) or by turning off the A87 at Ratagan. The Ratagan route is very steep, climbing to 400 metres from sea level. There is a hotel and a shop in Glenelg village.

Beyond this the road continues on to Arnisdale, giving great views over the Sound of Sleat to Bla Bheinn (927 metres) on Skye. As you turn the corner and go east towards Loch Hourn there is a great view of the island of Eigg. The mountains of the island of Rum stick up above Sleat on Skye.

As you turn east there are tremendous views across Loch Hourn towards the mountains of Knoydart.

LOCAL FACILITIES
There is a shop, a camp site and a tourist information office (01599-511264) at the junction of the Ratagan road and the A87. Ratagan has a youth hostel (01599-511243) and several B&Bs. It's possible to hire a boat to make the journey between Arnisdale and Kinloch Hourne (phone 01599-522353).

BORGIE FOREST

An easy bike route; good for children.

GENERAL NOTES
The rolling country, with its numerous lochs and lochans and wide, open spaces, has a certain charm on a fine day. There are some good quiet road options too, notably on the minor road from Skelpick and north of Borgie.

BORGIE FOREST
(9 miles)
This is marked with blue markers. The forest was one of the Forestry Commission's first plantings in 1920. It includes some 100-foot mature trees, remnants of a devastating fire years ago. Paradoxically, had it not been for the fire, these trees would have been cut down. Access is from the forest road a mile east of Borgie (not at the Borgie junction).

TRUDERSCRAIG
(NAVER FOREST)

An easy ride with archaeological interest.

GENERAL NOTES

This route isn't the most exciting in the world but the easy gradients make it a good option for families; it is educational, too, as there are a lot of archaeological sites.

TRUDERSCRAIG

(14 miles return distance)

This route starts from Rosal pre-clearance village in Strathnaver. This is just south of Syre on the B873. The route is signposted with red markers.

From the junction of the B871 and B873 take the B871 across the river, then follow the signs to Rosal village car park.

The forest road takes you past the Rosal pre-clearance village trail. It's worth briefly abandoning your bike to walk round the trail which explains what life was like in a highland village 200 years ago. The highland clearances in this area were among the most notorious, with thousands of people being cleared off lands where they had lived for generations – in favour of more profitable sheep.

The mountain-bike track to Truderscraig follows the River Naver south for three miles, then forks right at Dalharrold Farm. Here you cross open ground which gives good views of the hills and peatland of Sutherland.

After just over a mile you enter forest again and there is a final easy three miles to the end of the trail. Truderscraig pre-clearance village lies at the finish; leave your bike at the gate, as this is a protected archaeological site.

When Truderscraig Forest was being established, the surveyors discovered the remains of the village. To their credit, the Forestry Commission decided to preserve the site. The township covers 60 acres and records show that people lived there from 1269 until they were evicted in 1830.

When the Sutherlands bought their huge estates in the nineteenth century, the land around here was populated by thousands of families, descendants of crofters who had lived there for hundreds of years. The Sutherlands wanted their lands empty of people so that sheep could roam. They employed ruthless men to evict people from their homes, setting fire to them so they could not return.

The Clan chiefs, whom the people once might have looked to for protection, had now been seduced by the consumer society and had no ear for the cries of despair. An eyewitness in 1819 counted 250 crofts put to the torch in one night. All that's left now are sad piles of stones.

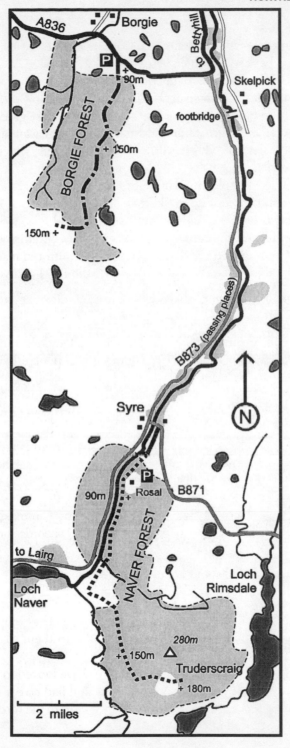

OTHER OPTIONS

There aren't any other marked mountain-bike routes close by, but there are some interesting back roads which you might like to try.

A mile south of the A836/B873 junction, a footbridge leads over to the hamlet of Skelpick. Cross this and you can bike most of the way to Bettyhill on a quiet back road.

Also on this road is the great burial cairn at Achcoillenaborgie, first used as a burial site 6,000 years ago. This has three burial chambers, which you can visit, in a cairn 70 metres long.

There's a scenic ten-mile circular route starting at Borgie (see map) which takes you via some fine beaches to Skerray.

Strathy Forest is ten miles east of Bettyhill. There are no marked trails but there are more than 20 miles of forest roads to explore. OS Landranger map sheet 10 would be required.

LOCAL INFORMATION

Bettyhill is a small, straggling village with a tourist information office (01641-521342), shops, etc.

Strathnaver Folk Museum, just east of Bettyhill, has a lot of material on the clearances as well as other matters of local history. Another famous item in the churchyard is the Farr Stone. This intricately carved cross dates from the ninth century; it's still in fine condition, as the rock the artist was working in a thousand years ago was hard schist.

ARDROSS FOREST

A long and a shorter route in varied forests near Tain.

GENERAL NOTES

This area is attractive because the forest is fairly broken up with lots of open areas. To the north these often give good views of the Dornoch Firth, and there is an attractive area here with lots of Scots pine poking through the heather.

The minor roads round about are quite quiet, and even the B9176 (formerly the A836) is fairly quiet, being bypassed by the new A9 which now crosses the Dornoch Firth.

Tain is an attractive old town with many fine Victorian buildings and a busy high street with a good tea room. Tourist information: 01862-892122.

The bike routes are fairly easy, being on forest roads with the occasional minor road. The routes are good for families.

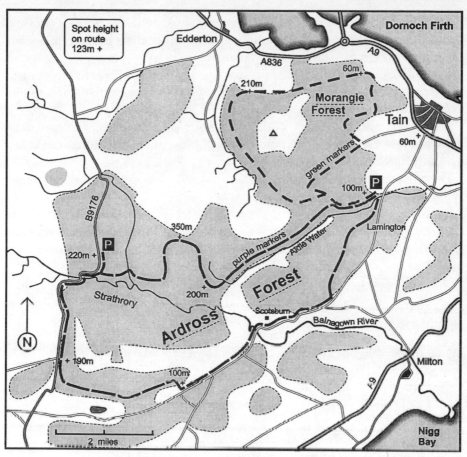

MORANGIE HILL ROUTE

(14 miles, green markers)

This is the easiest of the routes; none of it is on public roads. The simplest way to get to it is off the A9 where this bypasses Tain, signposted Scotsburn. Follow this minor road for just over a mile and you'll see the Forestry Commission car park.

Taking it clockwise, the route begins with a fairly flat section near Aldie Water, which is very pretty, then it turns north-west, starting a gentle climb.

The climb is quite easy, but it does last for about four miles so that at the end of it you are 200 metres above sea level. When the route curves round to the east you enter an open area and there are fine views over the Dornoch Firth.

There is a forest walk passing through here; you're not supposed to ride on the walking path. This area is not plantation forest with uniform spruce trees but a mixture of heather and Scots pine; it is a good spot for a picnic.

219

After this there's a fairly steep descent taking you to the eastern edge of the forest. Following this you turn south, then west, with another short but steeper climb to return to the start.

STRATHRORY ROUTE

(22 miles, purple markers)

This is, of course, longer and rather more difficult than the green route. You can start it from the same place, or from the Strathrory car park off the B9176. Most of it is off public roads, but there are three miles on the B9176 and four miles on a quiet minor road.

The B9176 is fairly quiet. It has some great views and steep hills, but these are mostly north of the part used by the mountain-bike route. At its south-west end the route is three miles from the town of Alness. Alness isn't a particularly attractive town to visit, though; Tain is a better choice.

Starting from the eastern Lamington car park, the route runs west by Aldie Water for four miles, climbing gently for most of the time. Following this the route loops north, climbing steeply at first.

After a little while this steep climb becomes easier and the route turns west again, descending to Strath Rory. After this you travel west for a further mile and join the B9176. Turn left here to continue the circular route.

You travel south on the B9176 for about three miles (this is mostly a descent), then fork left into the forest again – look out for the marker post shortly after a minor road junction.

Following this there is a fairly flat section where you travel east for three miles. This ends with a little descent on to a minor road; turn left here.

The minor road takes you north-east for about four miles; this is fairly flat and quite pleasant. You cross the Balnagown River, then, two miles after that and just after a road junction, you turn left to re-enter forest.

The final two miles are an easy climb, followed by an easy descent back to the Lamington car park.

KYLE OF DURNESS TO CAPE WRATH

This loneliest bike route is also one of the most interesting.

An 11-mile journey to the north-west tip of Scotland.

GENERAL NOTES

Despite the way it sticks out into the North Atlantic, Cape Wrath is not the most northerly point on the mainland; that distinction belongs to Dunnett Head.

Cape Wrath might be a mile or two further south, but the highest sea cliffs in mainland Britain are here, 280 metres high at nearby Clo Mor.

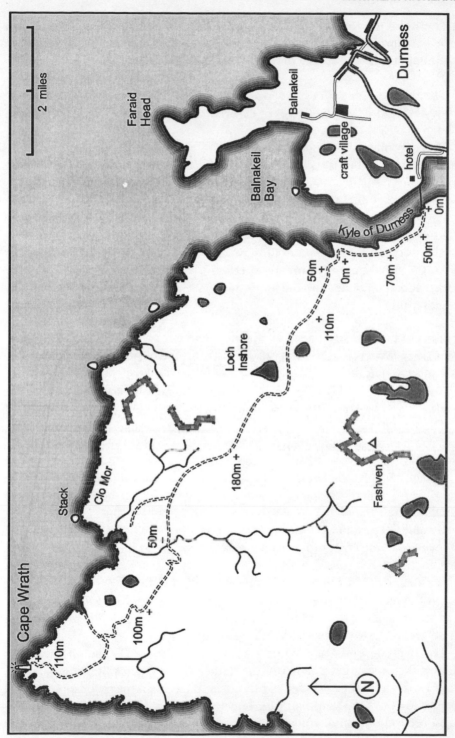

2 miles

Faraid
Head

Durness

Balnakeil

craft village

hotel

Balnakeil
Bay

Kyle of Durness

0m +

50m +

50m +

0m +

70m +

Loch
Inshore

110m +

180m +

Fashven

Stack

Clo Mor

50m

100m +

Cape Wrath

110m +

N

The route to Cape Wrath was at one time a surfaced road, but it's in such poor condition now that your average dirt road is often better. Perhaps it's cheaper nowadays to supply the lighthouse by helicopter than to maintain the road.

The track to Cape Wrath is separated from the rest of the road network by the Kyle of Durness; a foot-passenger ferry takes you over (it costs £3.50 with a bike).

The only other vehicle on the road will be a minibus that operates a shuttle service. The minibus is taken over by lighter at the start and end of the tourist season.

Bear in mind that there's no shelter of any kind along the way and that the route is very exposed. The weather can change very rapidly, so you must take adequate waterproof clothing.

The ferry service is frequent in summer, but because the Kyle of Durness is tidal, the ferry can only operate at certain times; phone 01971-511376 for information. Access is from the minor road just south of Durness. The hotel by the ferry provides teas.

KYLE OF DURNESS TO CAPE WRATH

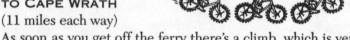

(11 miles each way)

As soon as you get off the ferry there's a climb, which is very steep at first but gradually gets easier until you are 70 metres high after travelling a mile.

There's a great view over the Kyle of Durness towards Balnakeil; following this you plunge to sea level again to cross a little bridge over the Daill River, before turning west away from the sea.

The next climb is higher still, and just as brutally steep at first as the previous one. There's a bit of a respite at a couple of lochans, then a more gradual climb to 180 metres.

By now the terrain has opened out. You pass quite close to the conical hill of Maovally and the crags of Fashven are clearly visible to the south. Shortly after this another track runs down to an attractive beach at Kearvaig. There is an interesting rock stack here, Clo Kearvaig (Cathedral Rock).

On the main route there's a gradual descent to cross Kearvaig River. After that the remaining four miles to the lighthouse are not too difficult, although there are a couple of steep little hills along the way.

The lighthouse at Cape Wrath was completed in 1825. The engineer was Robert Stevenson, grandfather of the author Robert Louis Stevenson. At the time I write it is still a manned lighthouse and has been manned from that day to this. By the time you read this, however, the lighthouse keeper will have been replaced by automatic machinery. Nowadays supplies are taken to the lighthouse by helicopter, rather than by boat and horse and cart from the Kyle of Durness.

The lighthouse consists of a 20-metre-high tower on top of a 102-metre cliff. It gives a flashing white light every 30 seconds or, in fog, a six-second blast every 90 seconds. Naturally, it's a listed building of historic and architectural interest.

If you look east you should be able to see the high cliffs at Clo Mor, as well as the rock stack Clo Kearvaig. If it's windy you'll have had a tough journey, but the surf on the rocks below will be impressive.

The return journey to the Kyle of Durness should be much quicker. You did remember to check on the return ferry times, didn't you?

LOCAL INFORMATION

Durness is strung out along the cliff top. There is a choice of shops and a good supermarket.

The youth hostel (01971-511244) is east of the village, just before Smoo Cave. Smoo Cave is in fact three caves, one including a waterfall. Walking access is to the first cave only, but you can see the second from a platform. To get beyond this you have to use a boat. You can get more information at Durness Tourist Office (01971-511259), who can also help with accommodation.

Another place worth visiting near Durness is Balnakeil Craft Village. This is not particularly attractive on the outside, as it consists of a collection of concrete huts (the leaflet says 'imaginatively converted from a military base'). Inside, though, you will find potters, weavers, enamelworkers, leatherworkers and other crafts people. There is also a coffee shop with home baking. It is a great place to spend some time if it's raining! Also quite near is Balnakeil Church, an interesting ruin.